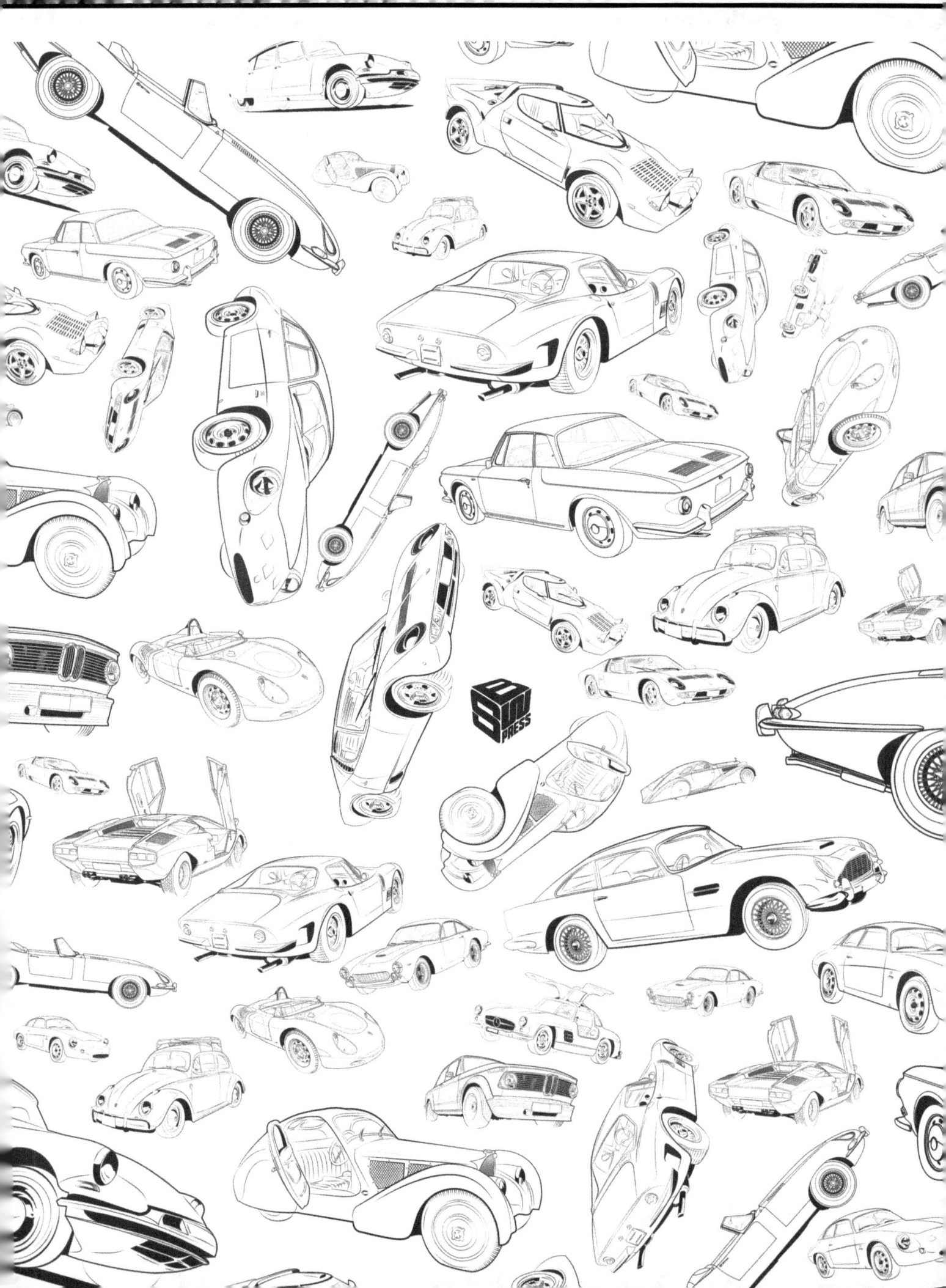

Inside the Lines:
European Icons

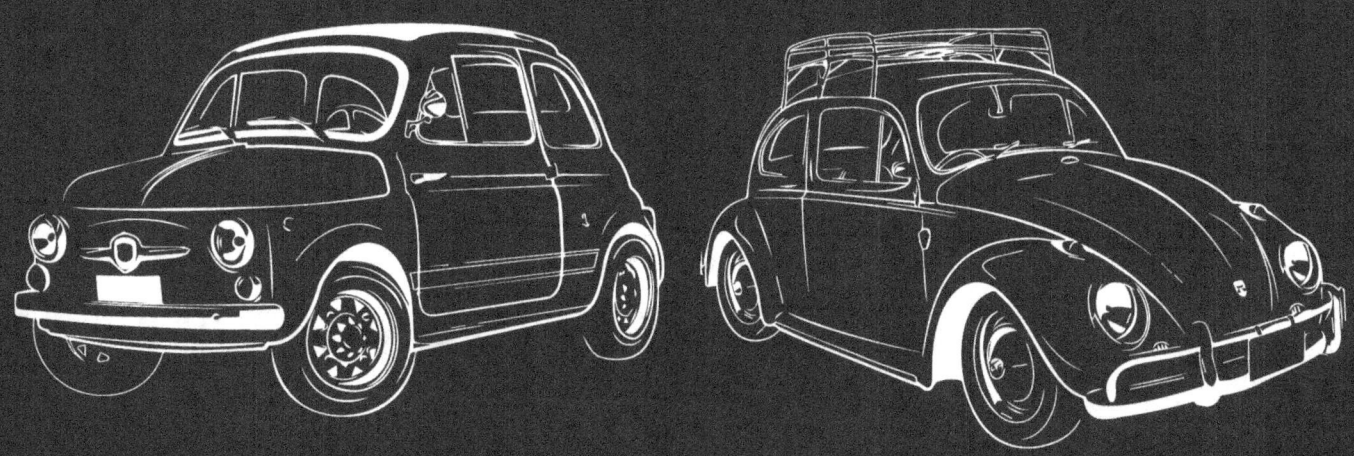

By Brandon & Steve Wilcox

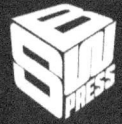

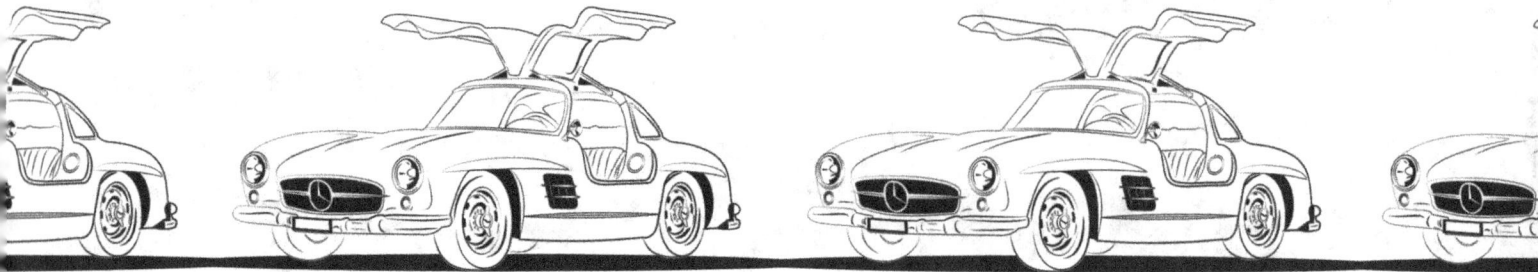

B S W   P R E S S
An imprint of sDub Concepts USA
www.sdubconcepts.com

ISBN 978-1539841470

Printed in the USA

Interior designed by Steve Wilcox

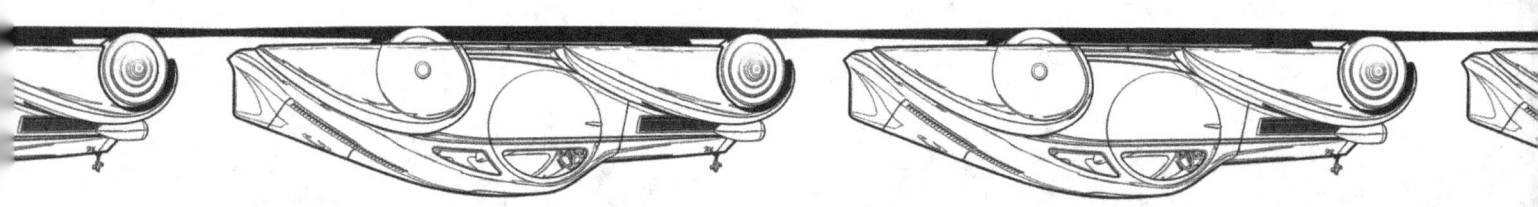

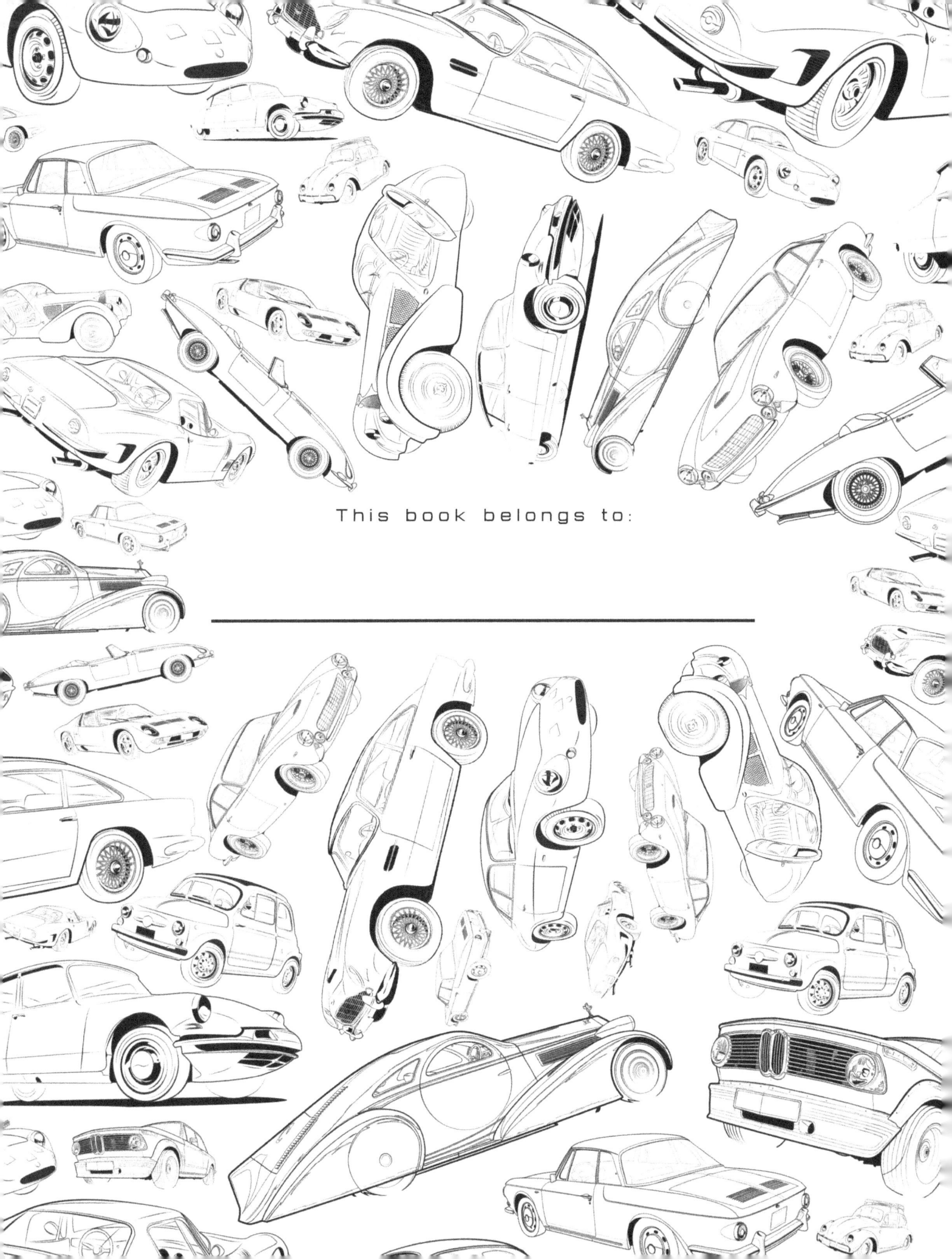

This book belongs to:

_____

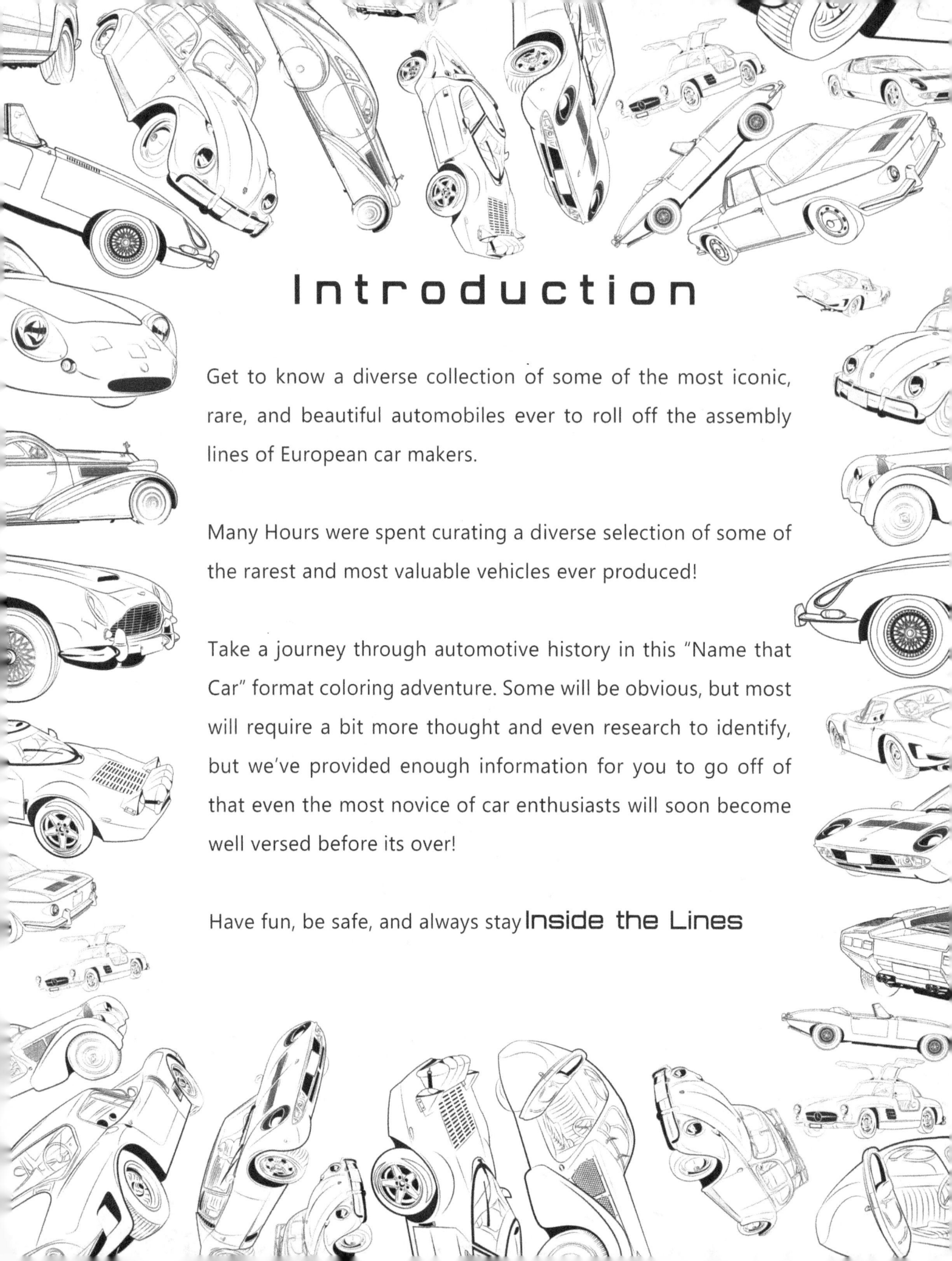

Introduction

Get to know a diverse collection of some of the most iconic, rare, and beautiful automobiles ever to roll off the assembly lines of European car makers.

Many Hours were spent curating a diverse selection of some of the rarest and most valuable vehicles ever produced!

Take a journey through automotive history in this "Name that Car" format coloring adventure. Some will be obvious, but most will require a bit more thought and even research to identify, but we've provided enough information for you to go off of that even the most novice of car enthusiasts will soon become well versed before its over!

Have fun, be safe, and always stay **Inside the Lines**

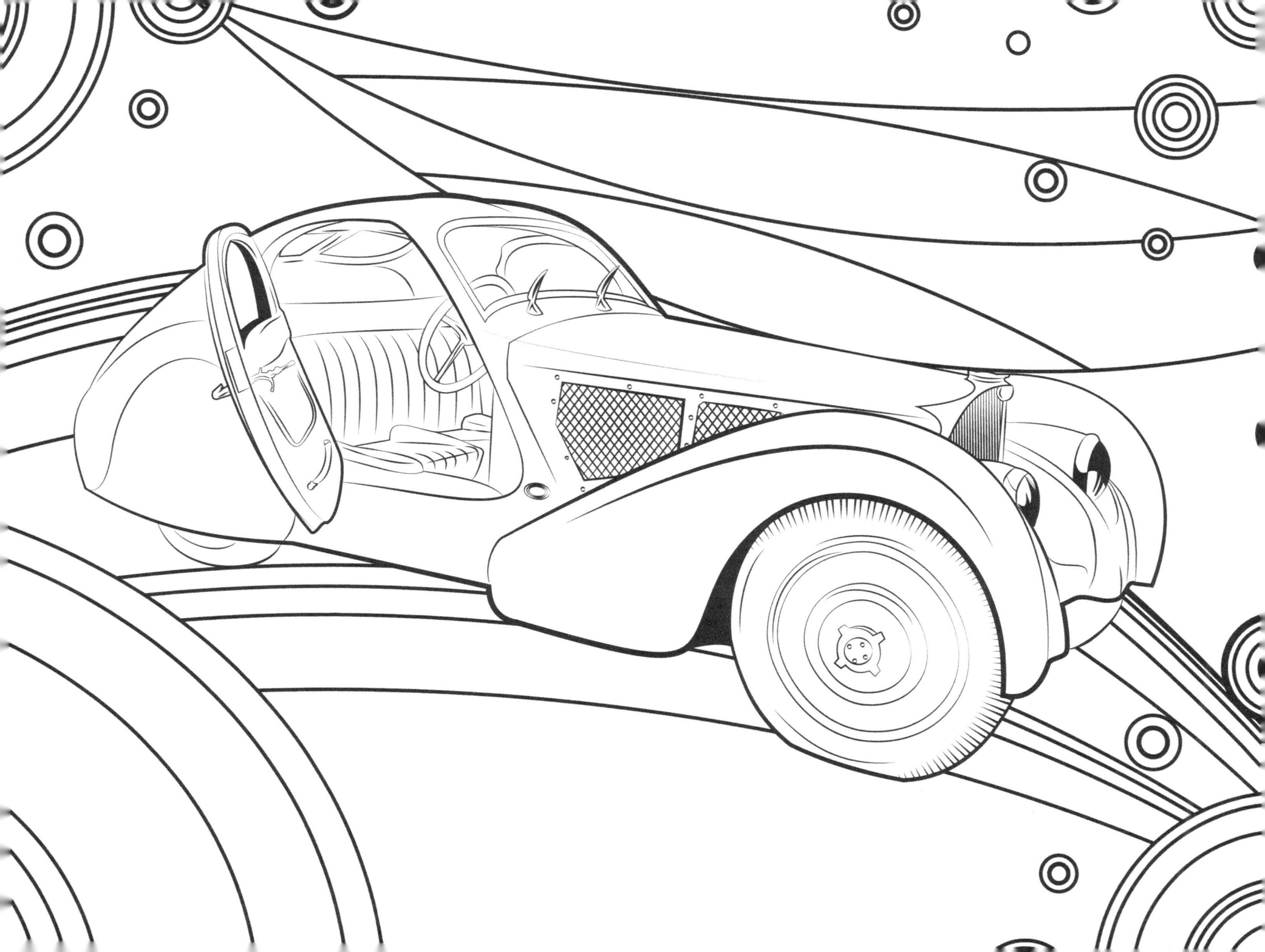

Built strictly for Grand Prix racing, its twin cab 8 cylinder engine elevated the company to its first major win in 1931. It's unique appearance is looked upon as automotive iconagraphy today.
- top speed: 140mph
-current value: $1-4.5 million

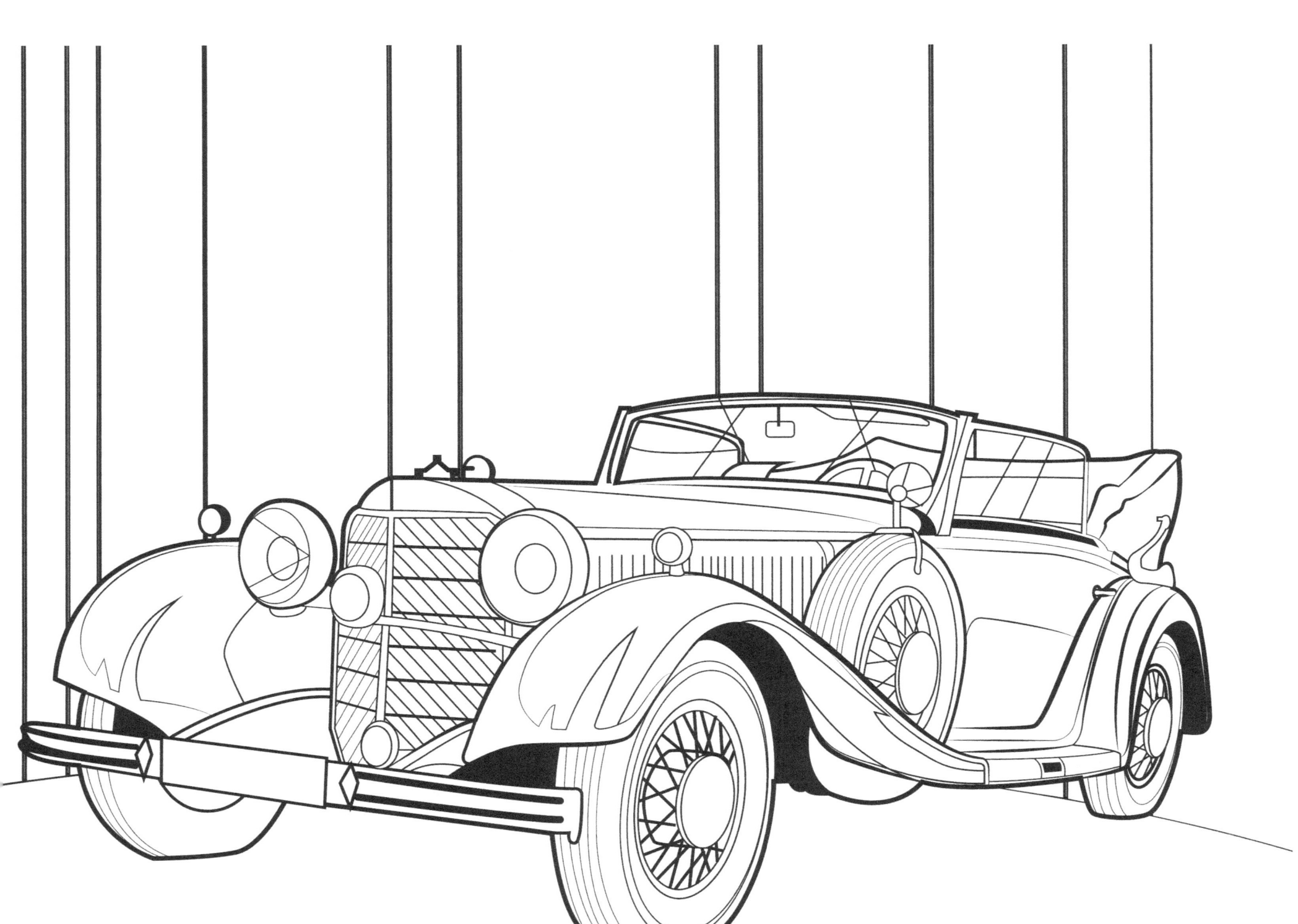

Can you name this German icon? Prized for its heritage and scarcity, only 122 units were ever produced. Known for its powerful engine and lavish couch work, the company delivered both greater luxury and performance then ever before. Today this classic convertible may cost you nearly $1.5 million USD.

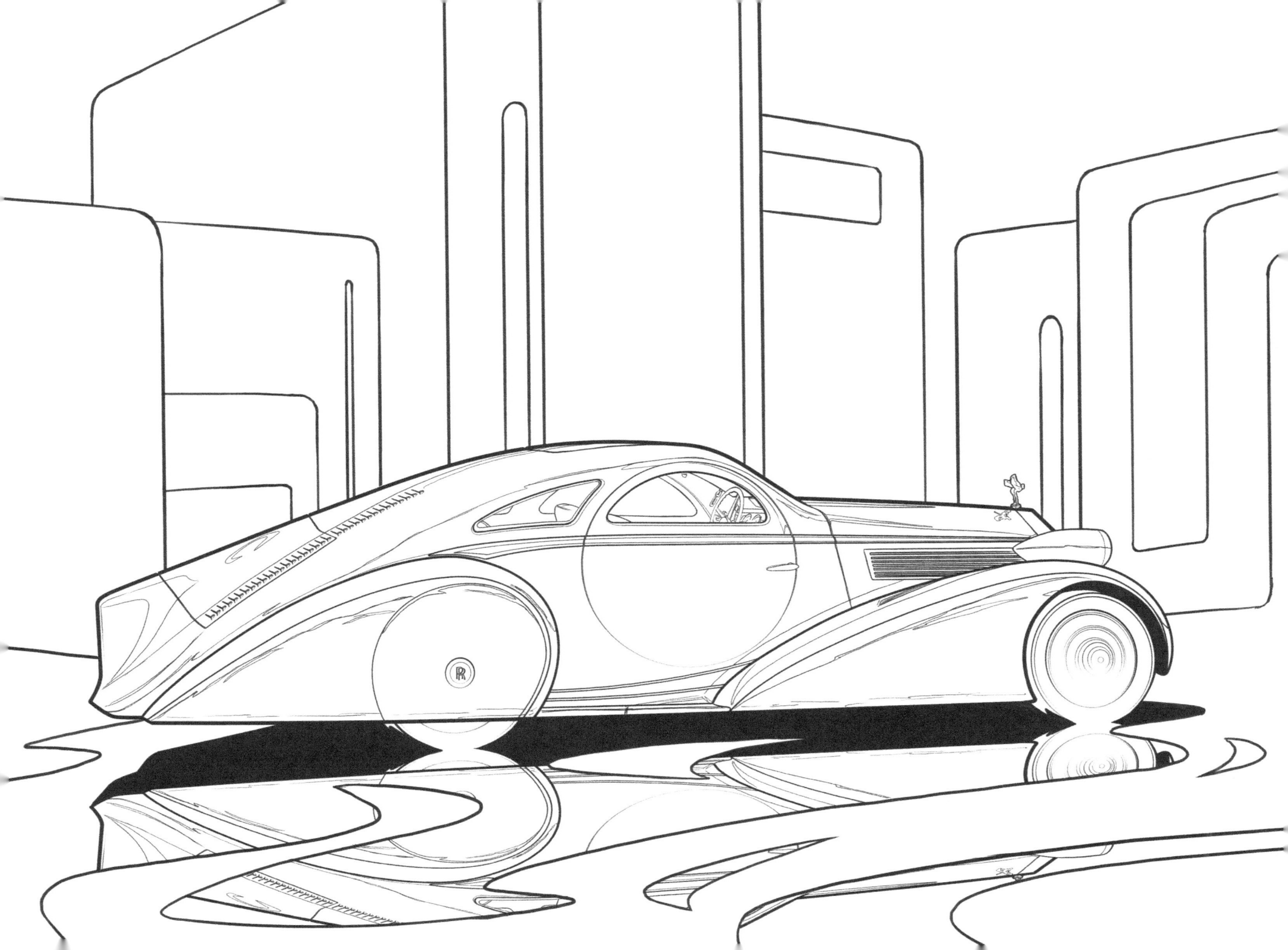

Not to many cars are as menacing and dramatic as this classic. It's stature and powerful curves are as intimidating as they are beautiful. Visually stunning with its oversized grille and circular doors, this is the classic of all classics. Can you name this icon?
Hint: Nickname, 'Round-Door Rolls'
Current value: over $1.5 million USD

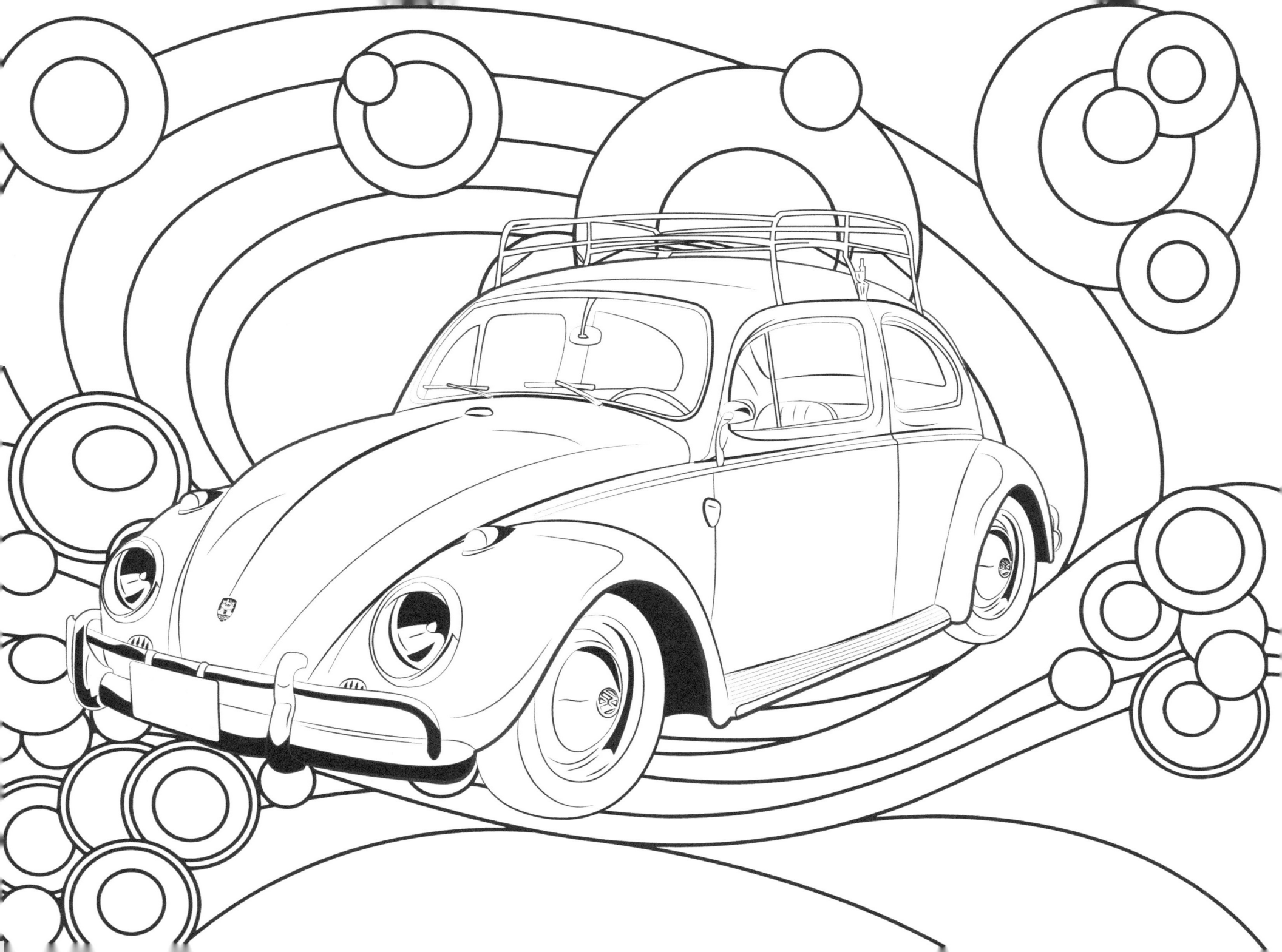

Possibly the most recognizable car in the world, it is one of the most interesting vehicles ever. Created by the need of a cheap functional car to be mass produced in Germany, Adolf Hitler formulated its production. The Beetle is the longest running and most manufactured car ever made with 21,529,464 units produced. Do you know its actual model name?

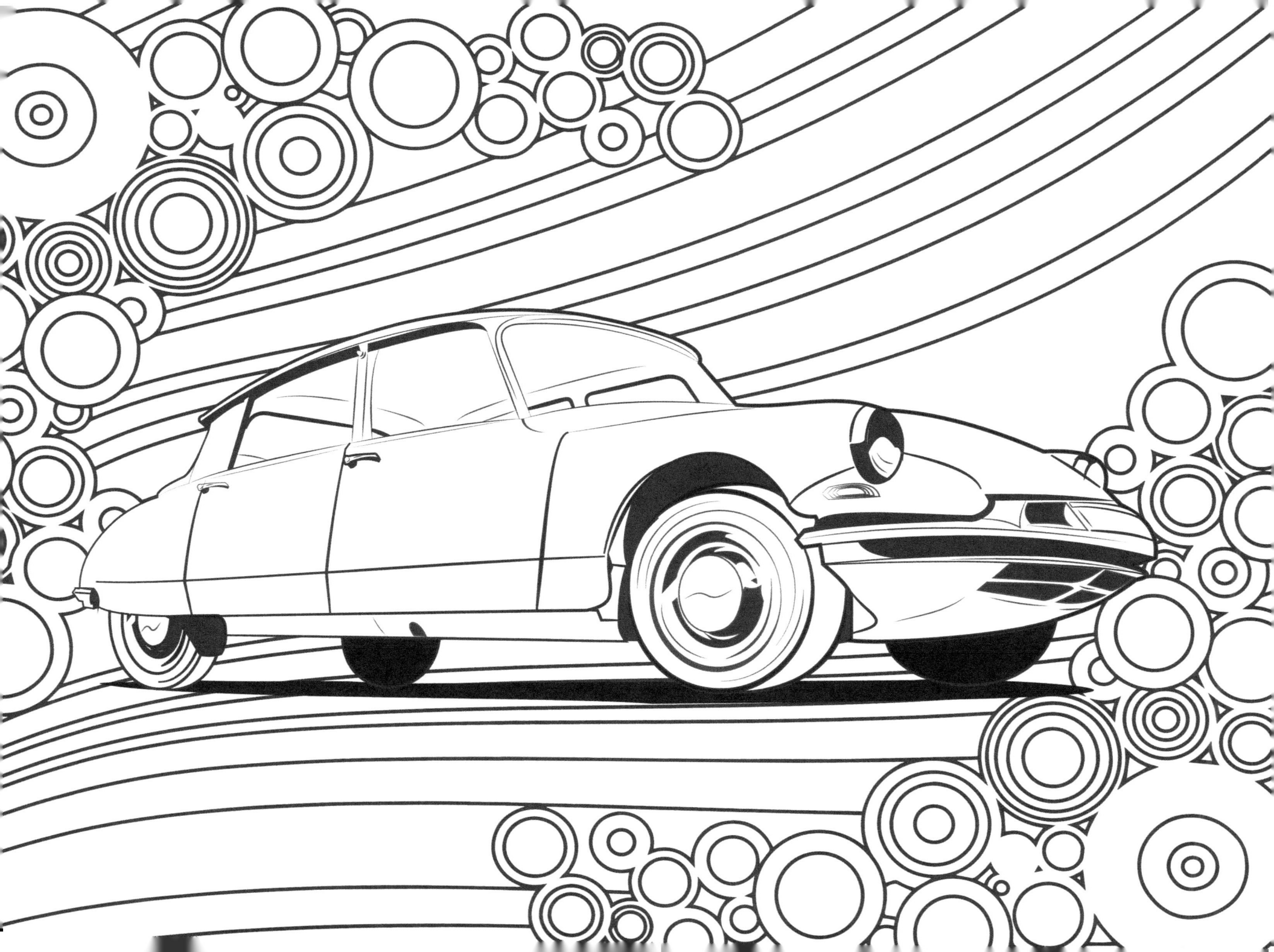

Known for its futuristic design and innovative technology this model set new standards in ride quality, handling, and braking. Focused on function and style it became the most successful vehicle to ever come out of France and the first production vehicle with hydraulic suspension frome the factory. Can you name it?

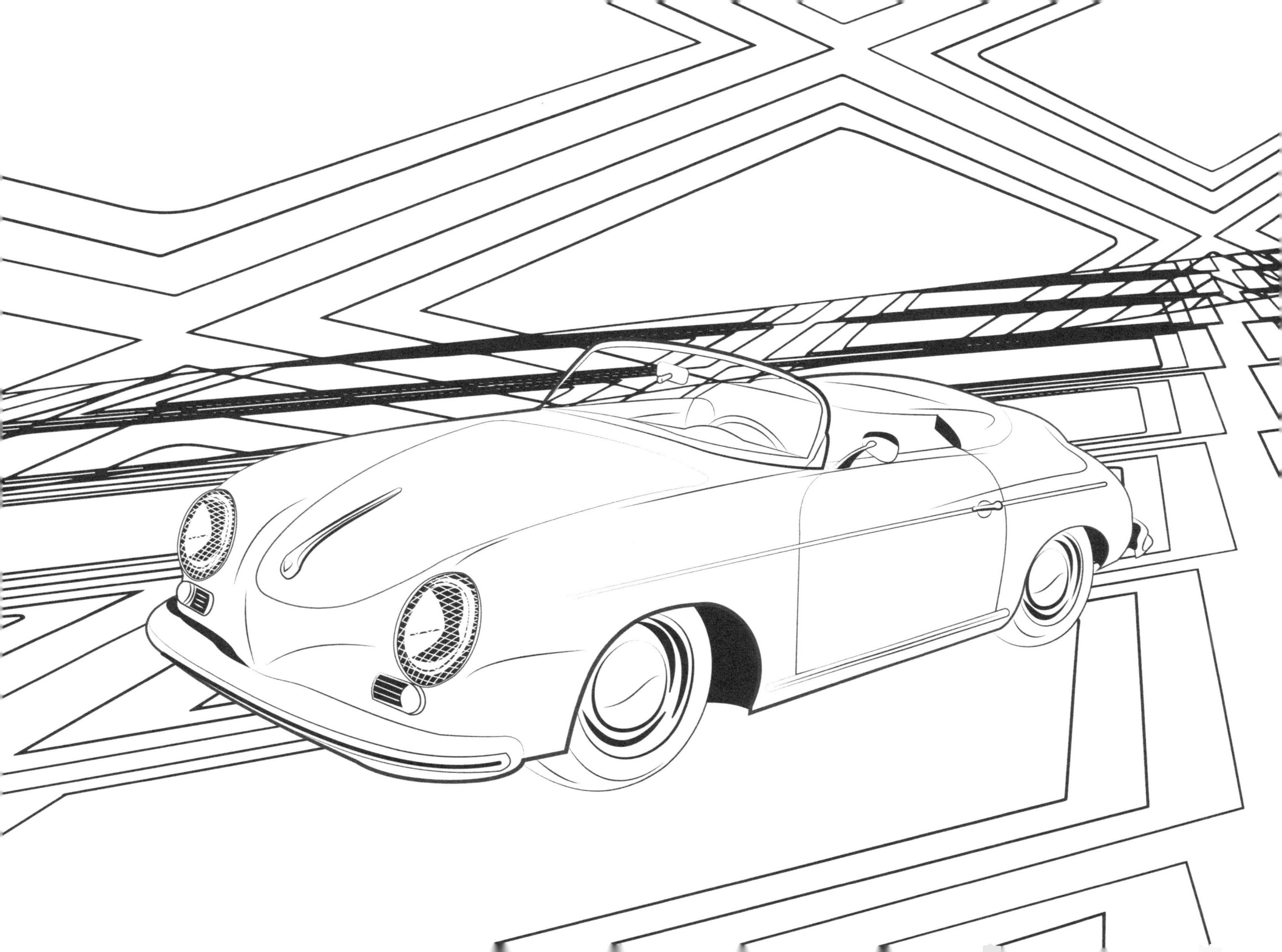

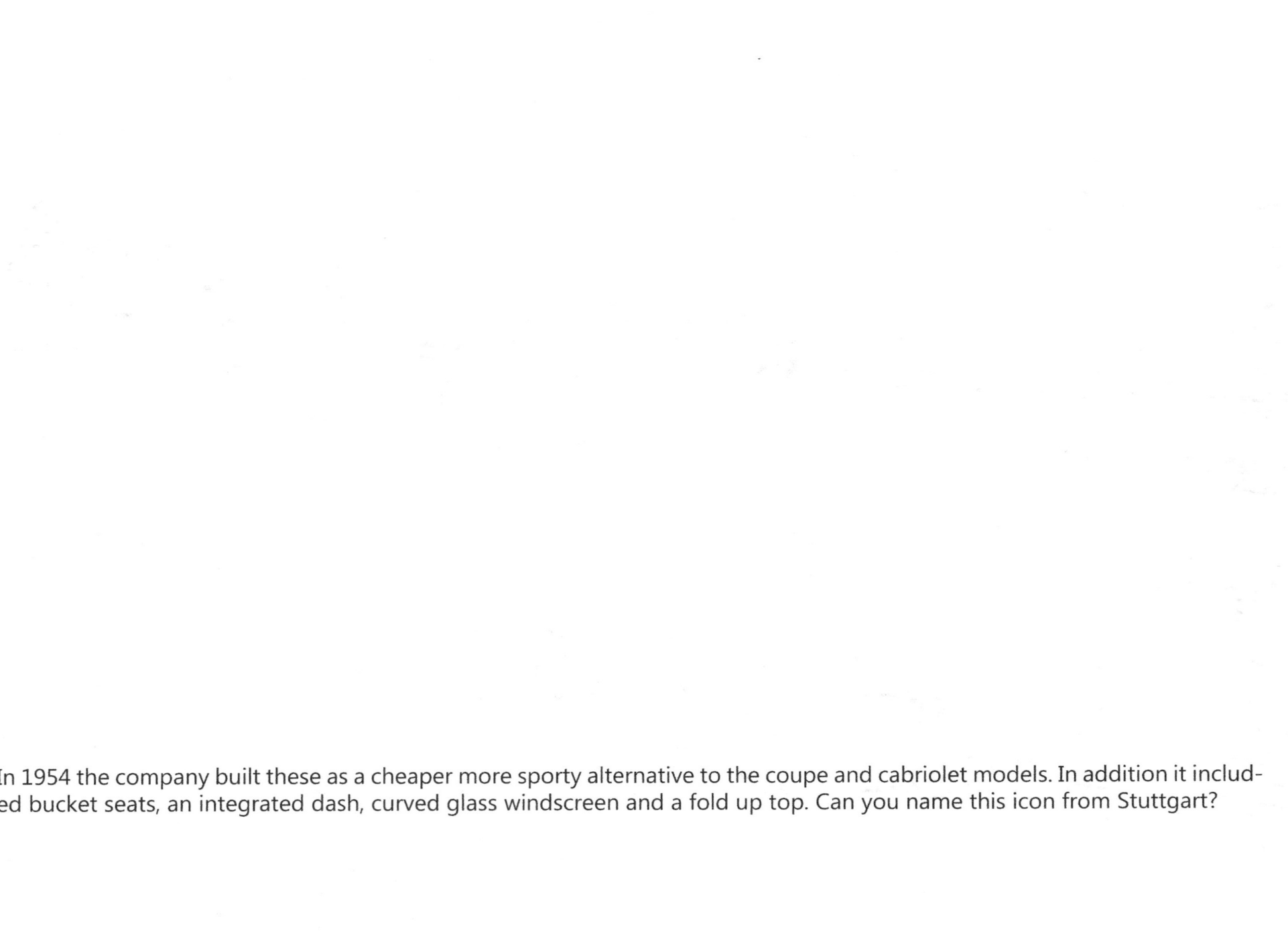

In 1954 the company built these as a cheaper more sporty alternative to the coupe and cabriolet models. In addition it included bucket seats, an integrated dash, curved glass windscreen and a fold up top. Can you name this icon from Stuttgart?

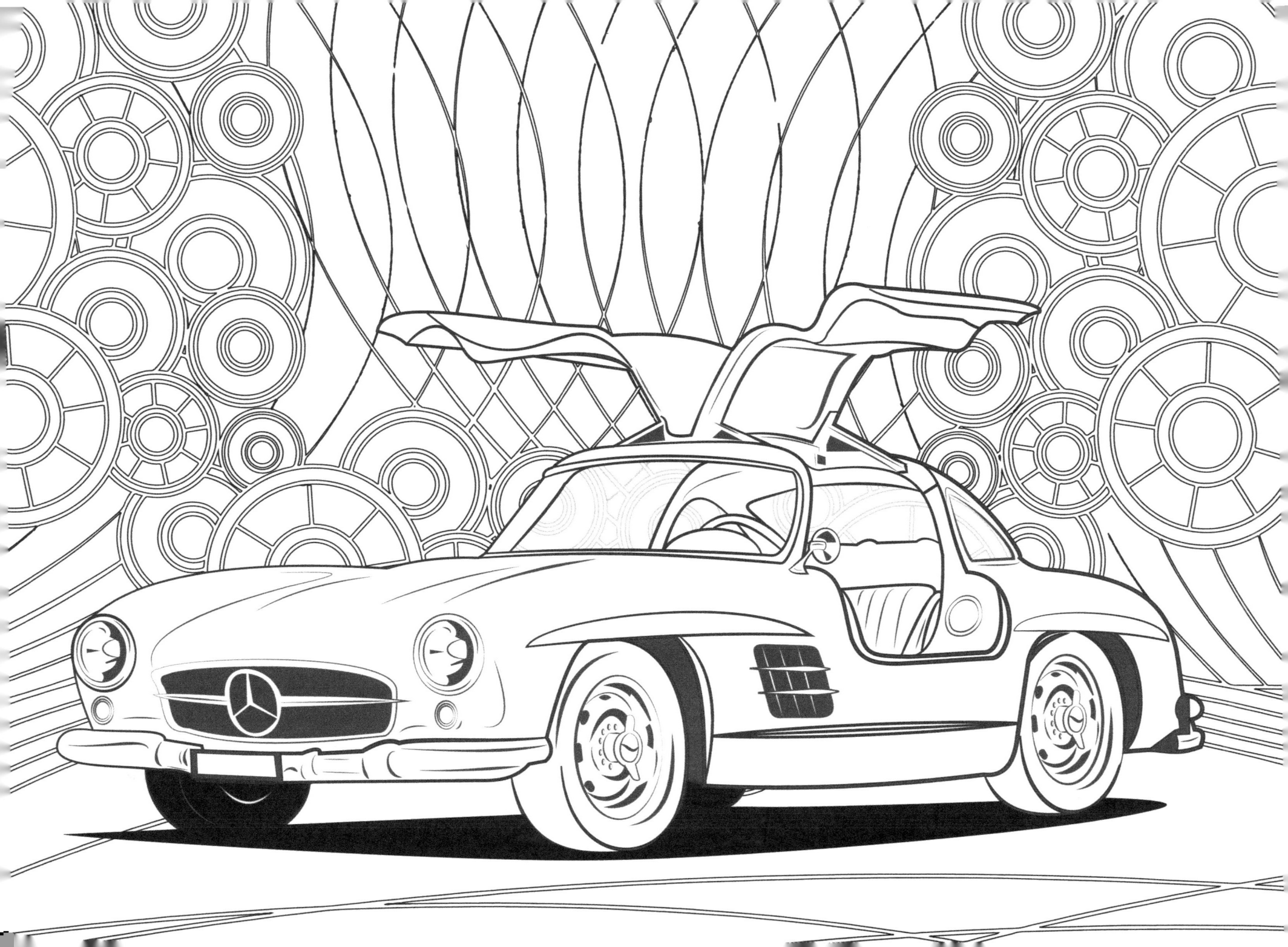

This model is considered as one of the most collectable vehicles ever and regarded as one of the top five sports cars of all time. In its day it was groundbreaking. Introducing the world to direct fuel injection, aluminum lightweight body, as well as the first gullwing veritical doors. Only 29 units were ever produced and one sold in 2012 for $4,620,000 USD.

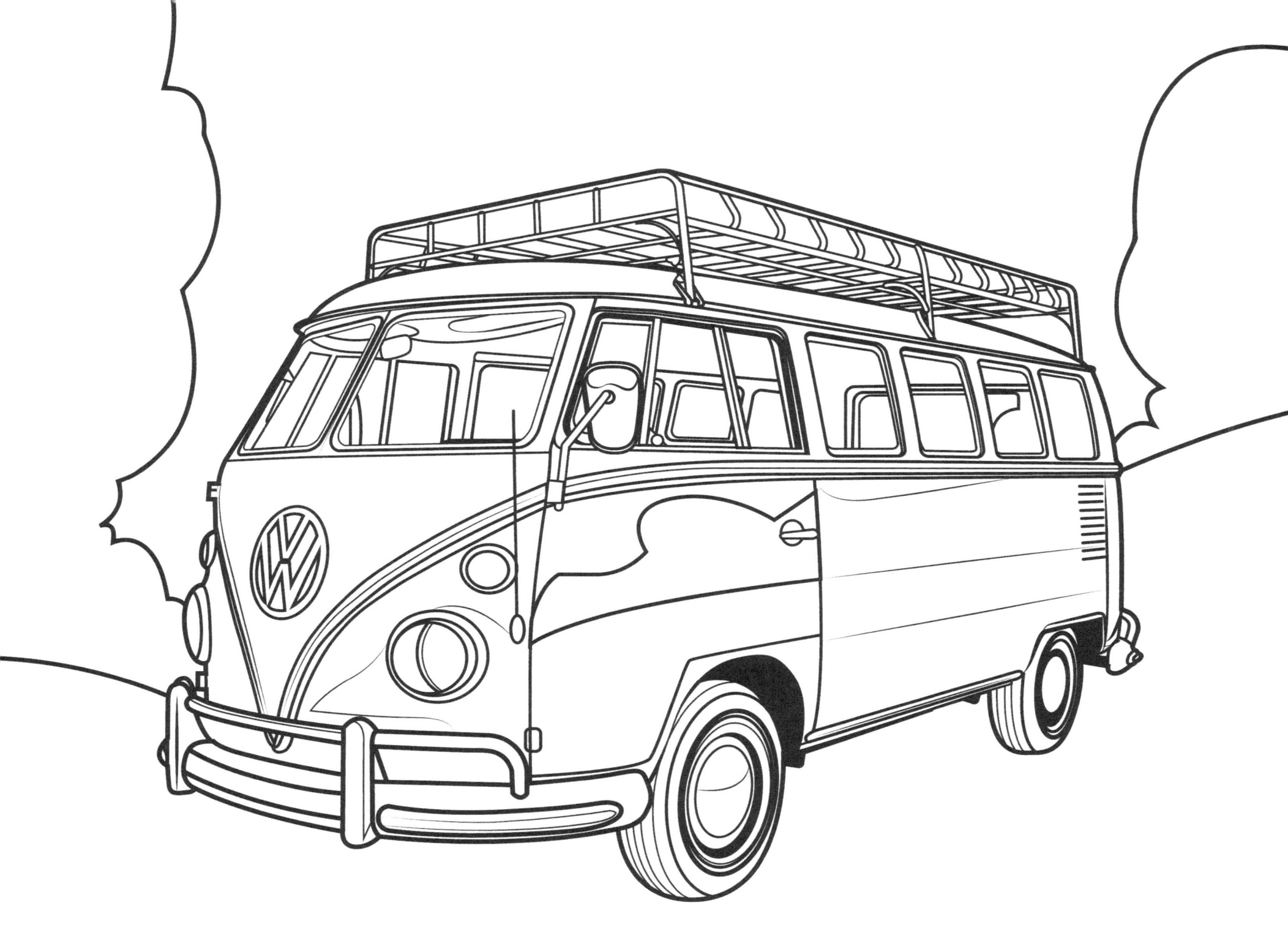

Can you name this icon? The car with many names. Microbus, minibus, hippy van, hippy wagon; these are just a few of the many nicknames given to the companies 2nd production vehicle. Made popular during the counterculture movement in the 1960s, the bus has grown into an icon today.

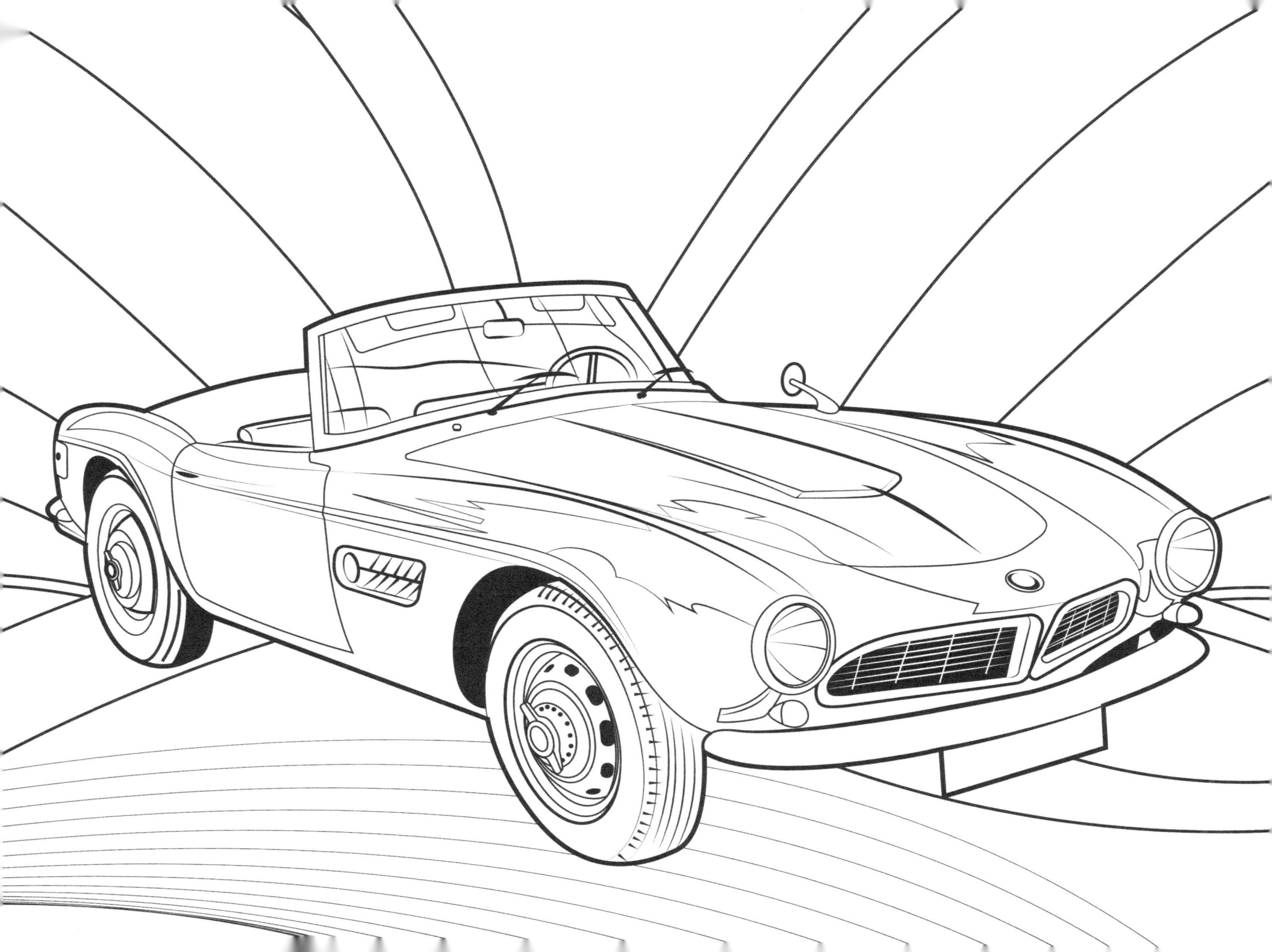

Name this vehicle! Intended to revive the companies sporty image, this model nearly left them bankrupt. Yet it's design was a milestone for the company, later influencing many later designs with its chrome side vents and horizontal front grilles. Uniquely, the 2 door convertible had a hand formed aluminum body so no two models were exactly the same.

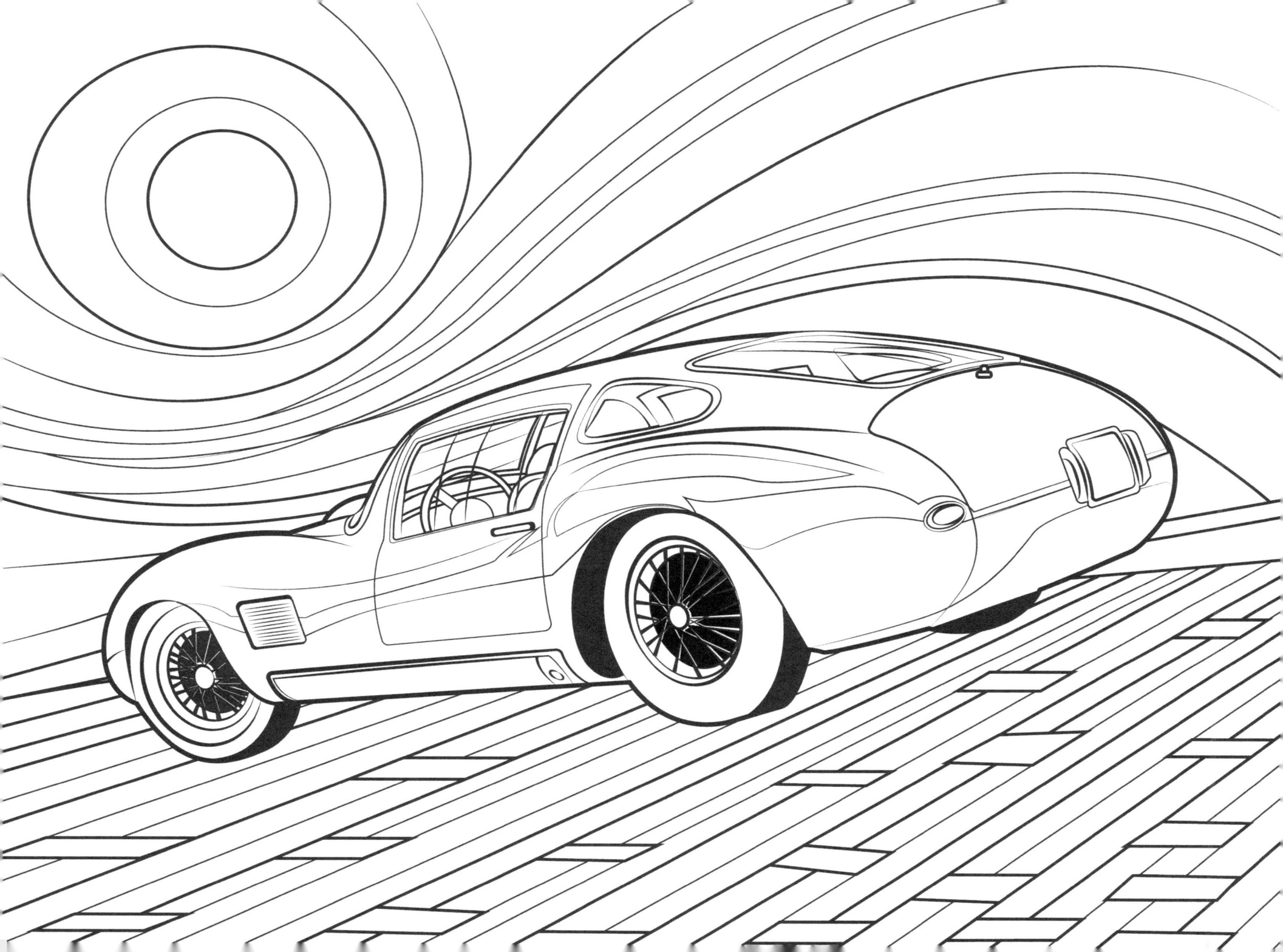

Deemed by many as the most beautiful car in history this uniquely designed supercar is the only one of its kind. Built to dwarf the competition in world racing championships, this V12 highly powerful racers biggest competition was itself, ultimately failing to win due to mechanical issues. Today it still is regarded as one of the greatest vehicles of all time. Can you name this classic?

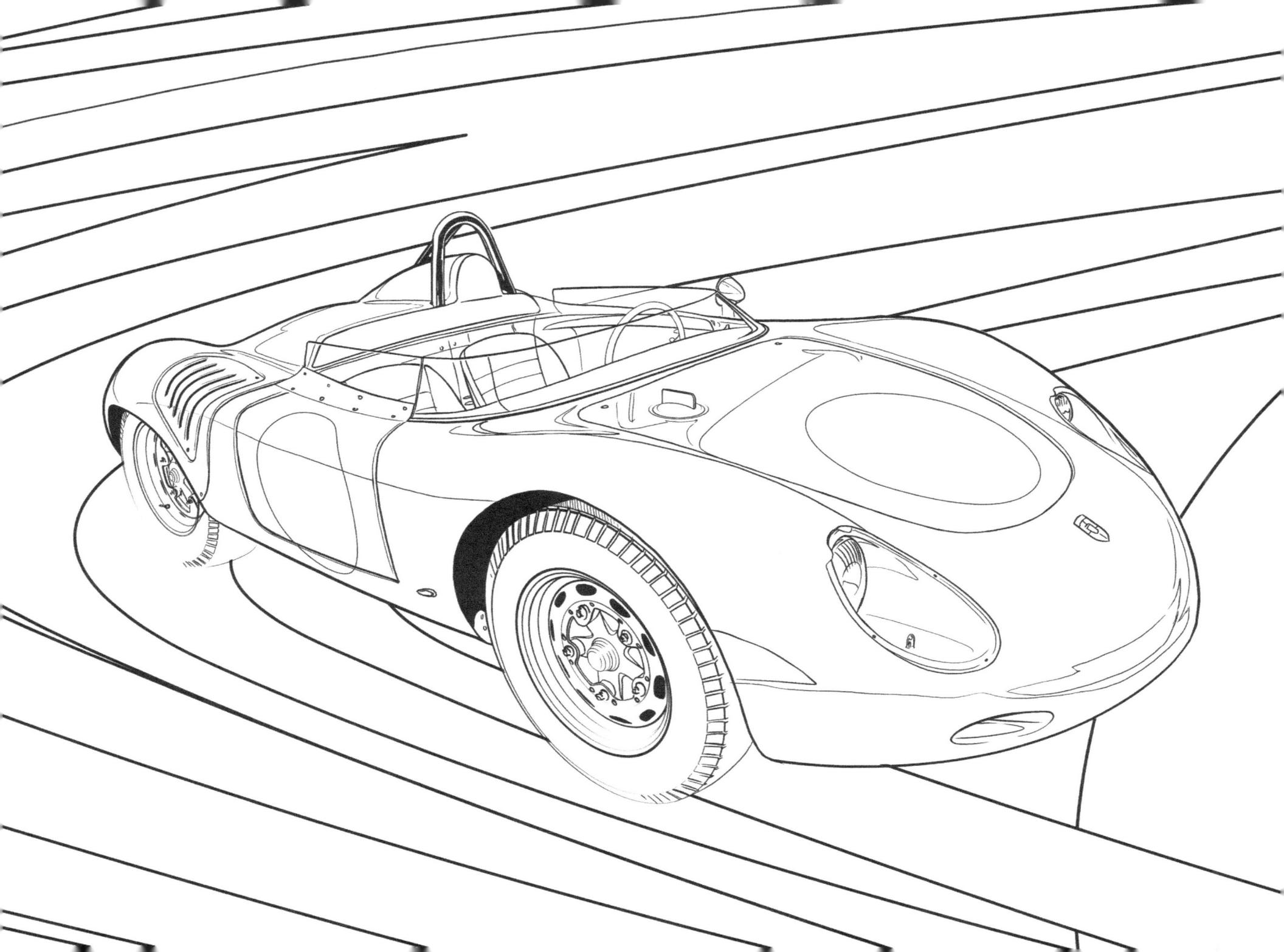

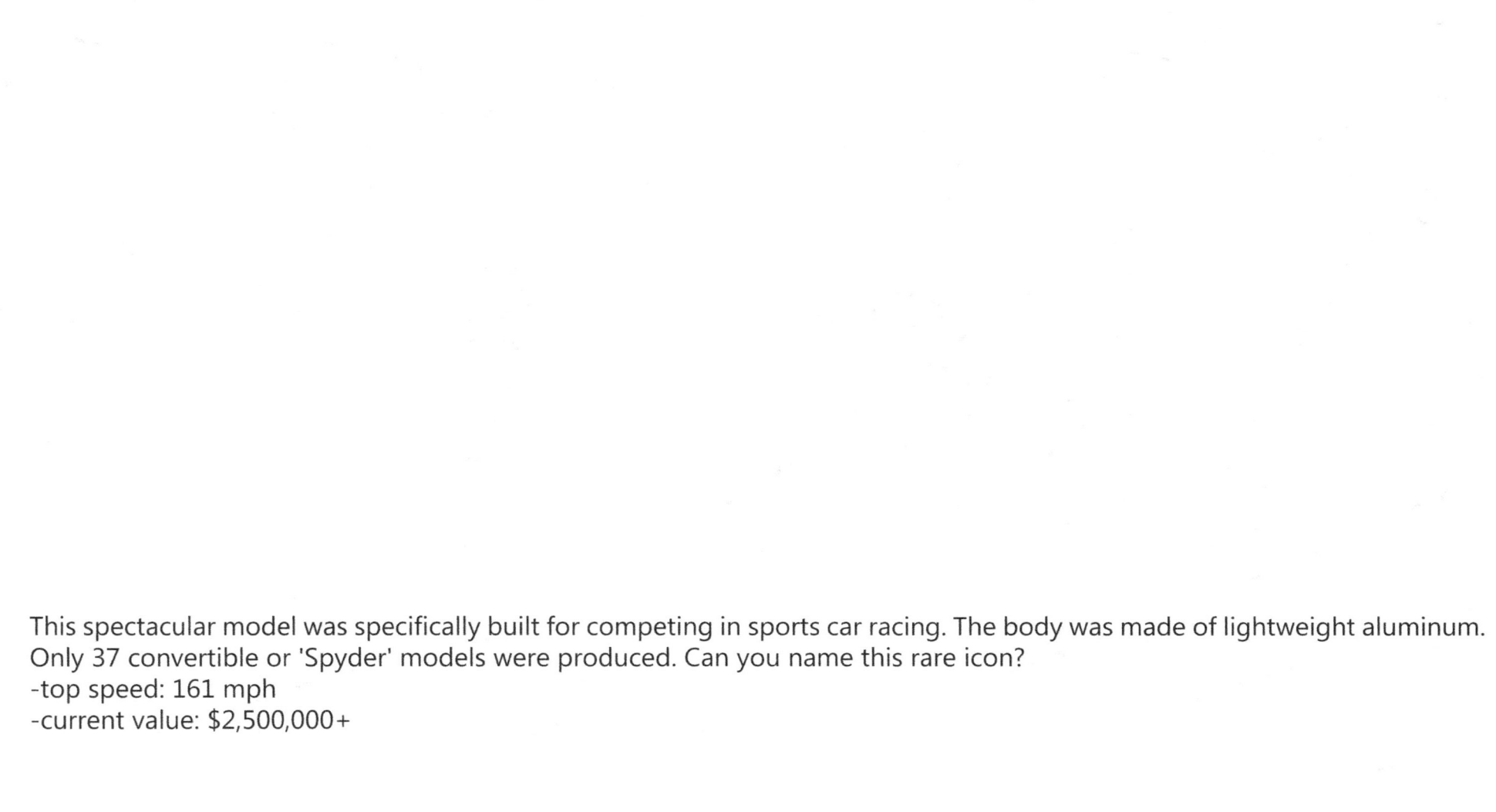

This spectacular model was specifically built for competing in sports car racing. The body was made of lightweight aluminum. Only 37 convertible or 'Spyder' models were produced. Can you name this rare icon?
-top speed: 161 mph
-current value: $2,500,000+

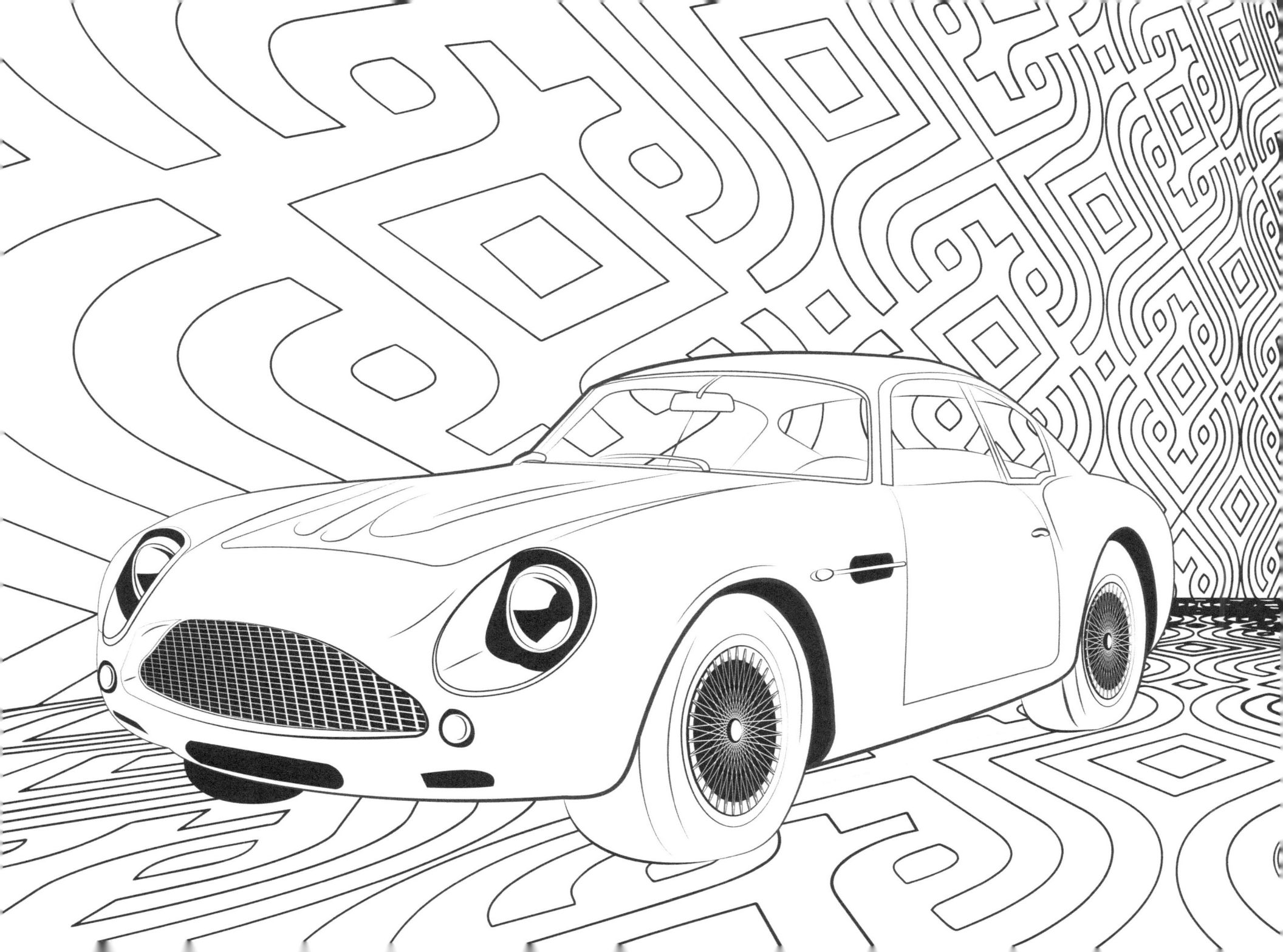

Name this Italian designed British masterpiece. It is hailed as one of the most beautiful cars ever produced and is also the most expensive British vehicle ever sold at over $10 million USD. Much of its body such as the bumpers were made aluminum to reduce the total weight.
- very rare only 20 units produced
- 0-60 time of 6.1 seconds
- top speed: 154 mph

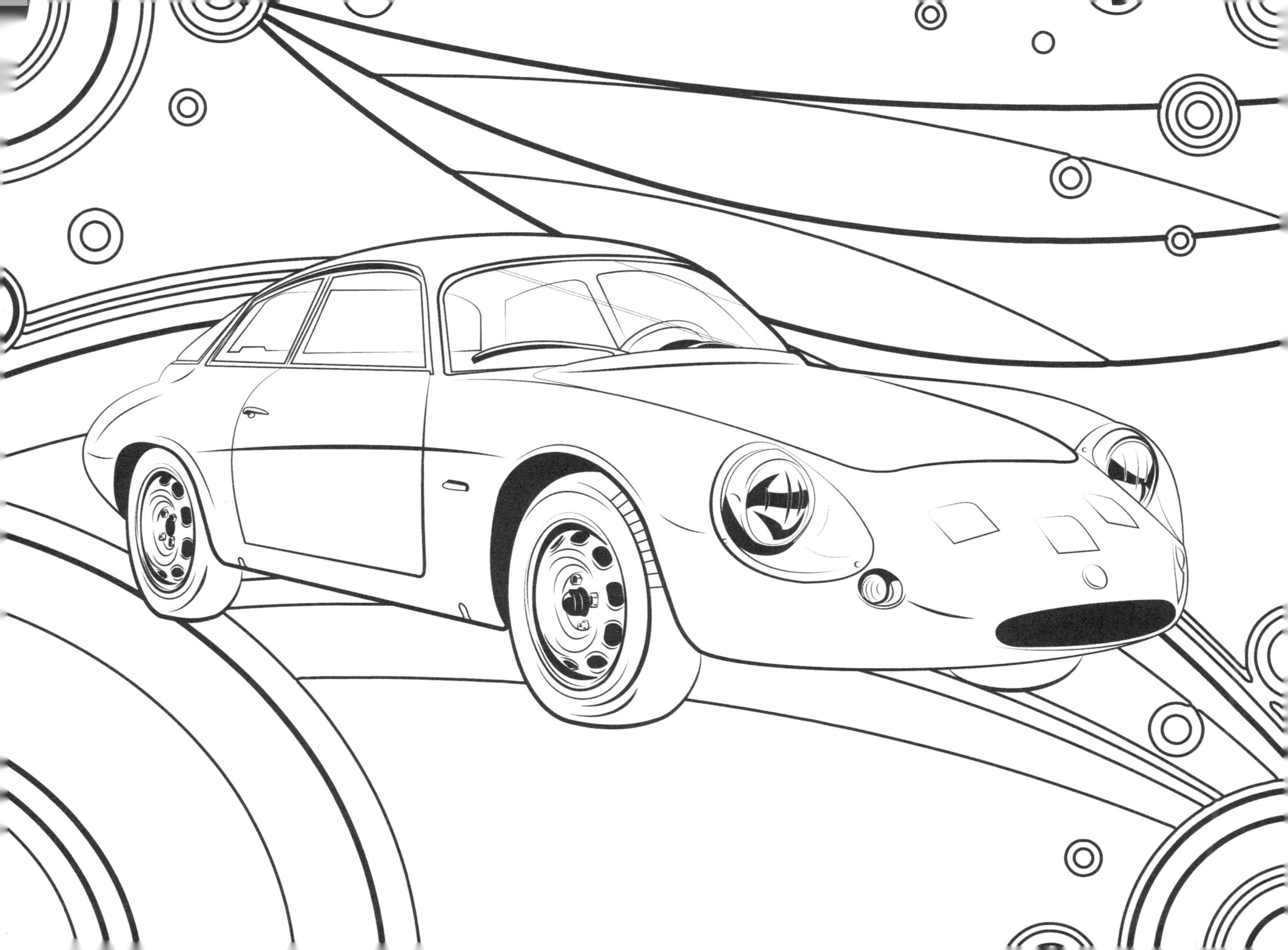

In 1961, only 30 units of this particular vehicle were produced. Its longer body, designed to be more aerodynamic, helped the Italian race car reach top speeds of 120 mph, impressive for its day. Today's value is roughly $300,000 USD. Can you name it?

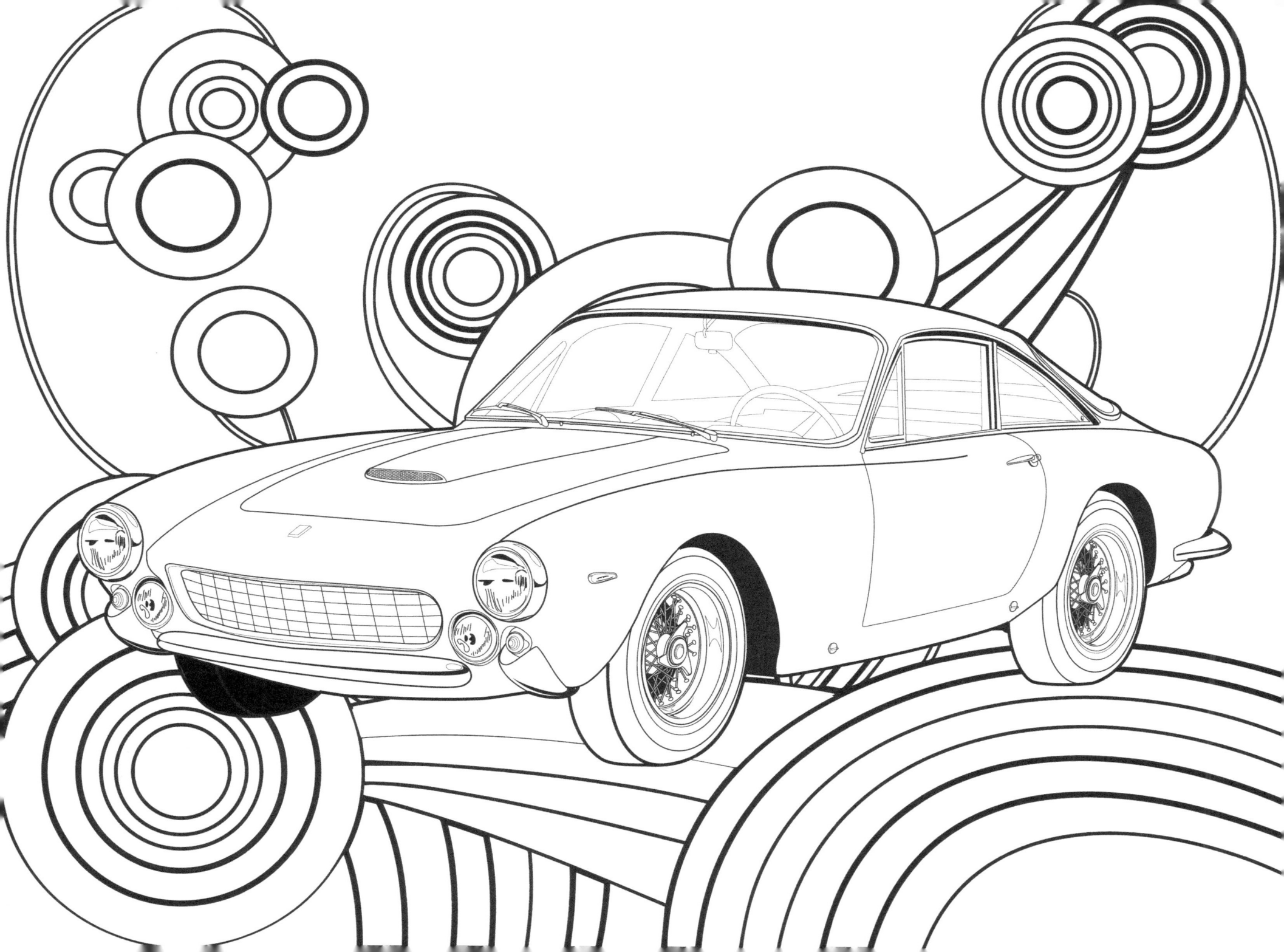

Widely considered to be one of the most elegant vehicles in history, this vehicle was built to meet the demands of those wanting something luxurious, comfortable and spacious while also getting a radical sports car. Equipped with a V12 engine it was the fastest passenger vehicle of its time and earns its classic reputation on all levels. Can you name this car?
- top speed: 150 mph
- 0-62 mph in 7 seconds
- sold new $13,000. current value $2million+

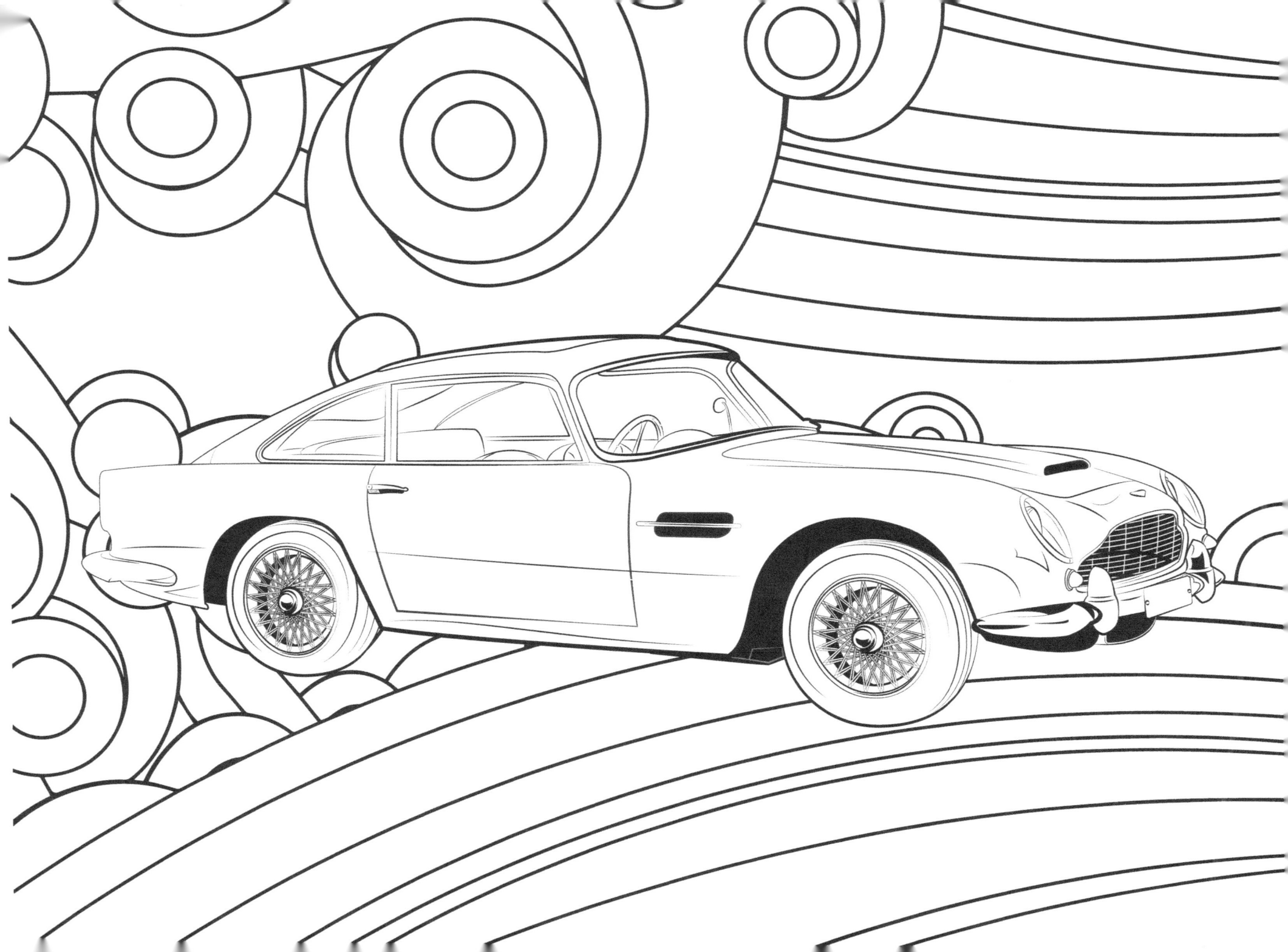

Can you name this sleek British classic? It's design was admired all over the world and was made popular by the James Bond films.
 -top speed: 139mph
- 0-60 9.3 seconds
- current value: $440,000+

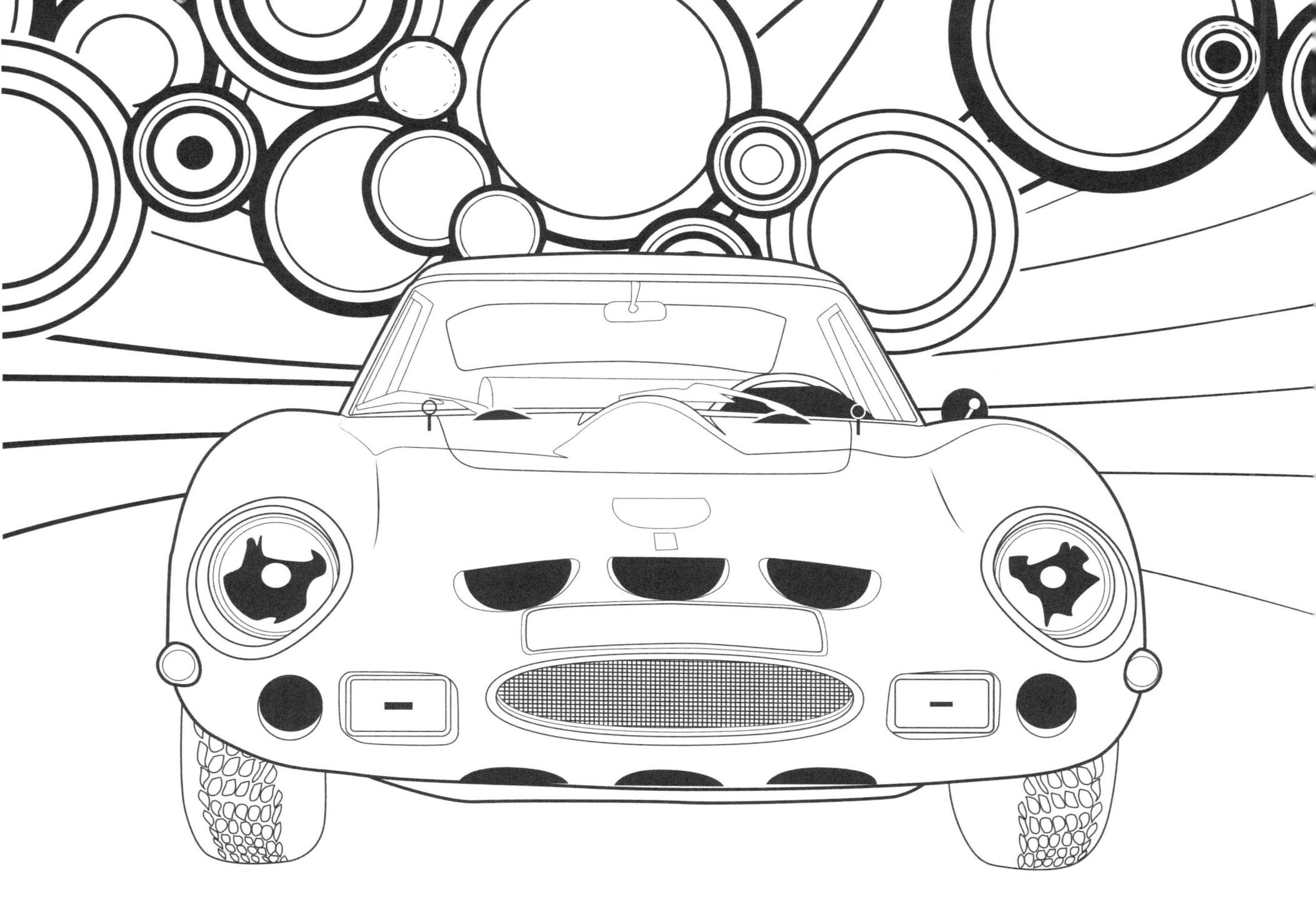

Name this rare Italian icon. Out of the 3 models ever constructed 2 were built with larger engines and competed in racing, while the third was constructed with a smaller engine for street use. Rare, fast, and extremely expensive, today's estimated worth stands at a whopping $30 million USD
- top speed: 158 mph
- 0-60 mph in 6.11 seconds

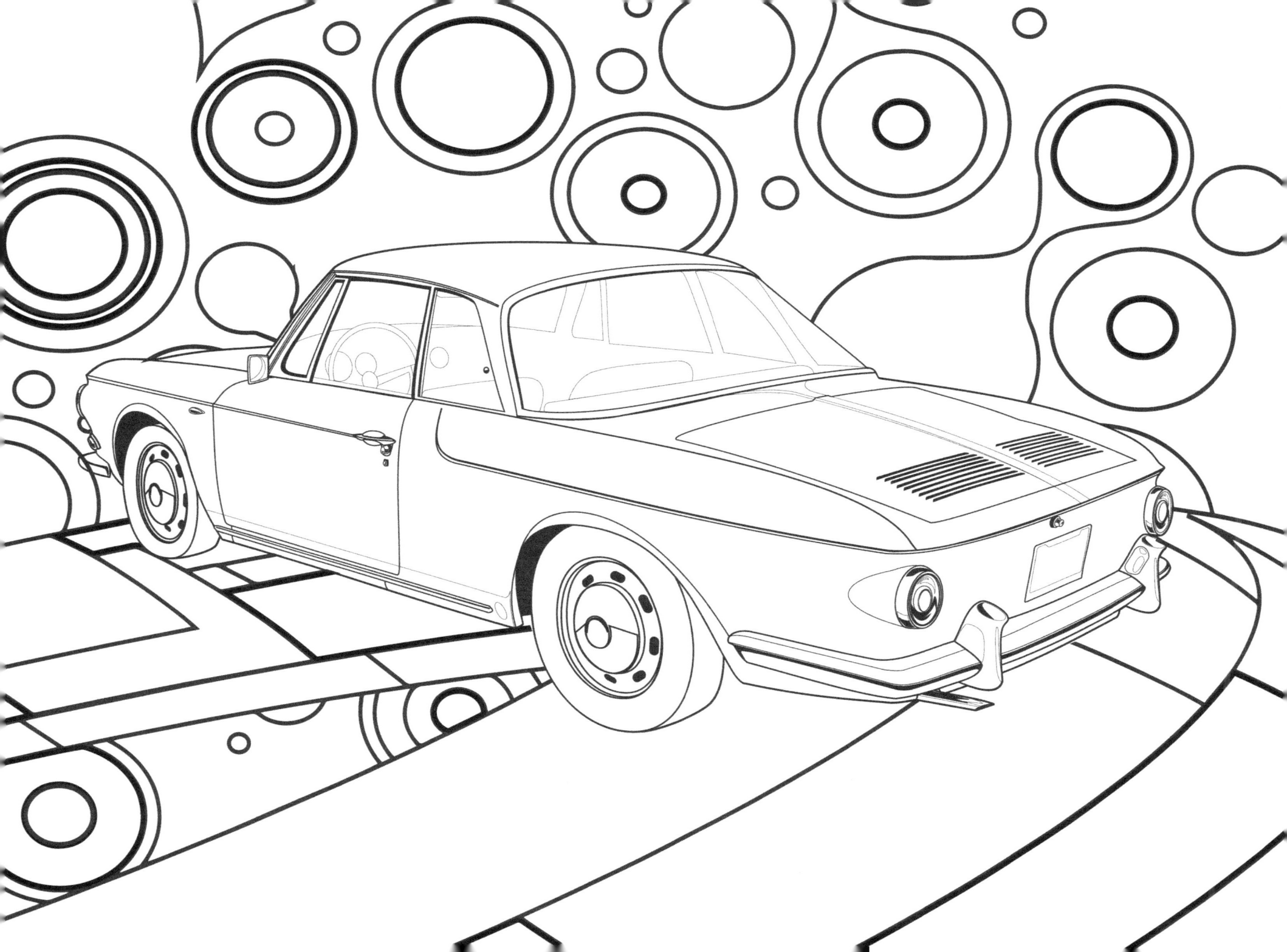

In 1962 this model added to the bodyframe of an already popular company model. With many more amenities including an electronically sliding sunroof and an upgraded engine, It was the fastest company car of the 1960s and cost nearly double the price of its other models.
-top speed: 137 mph

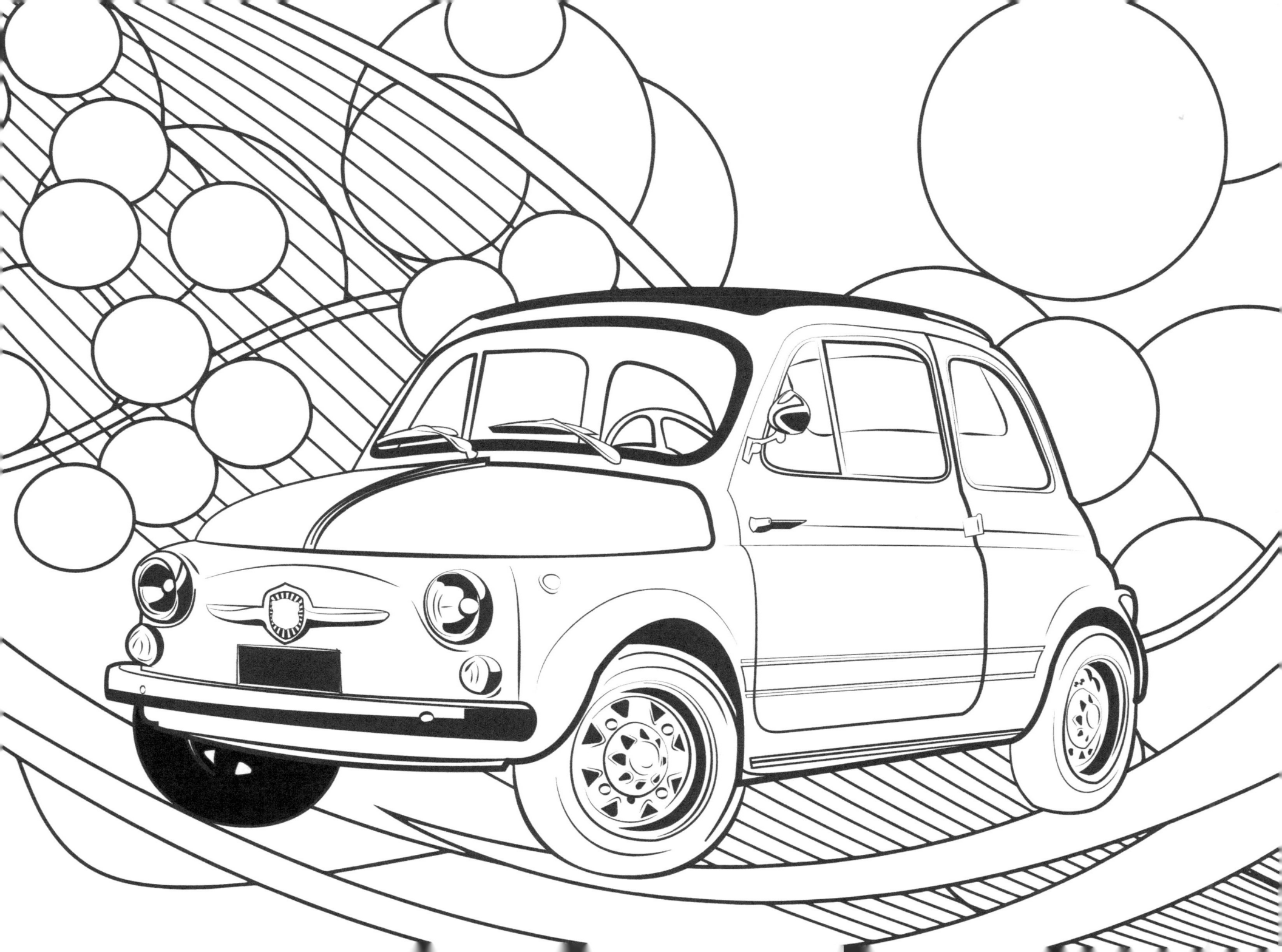

Name this two door, two cylinder "pocket rocket." The small size, great fuel economy, style, competitive price and friendly driving characteristics of its predessor just needed a cost effective performance boost. In 1963 this model added 8 horsepower and took the top speed from 62 to 75 mph.

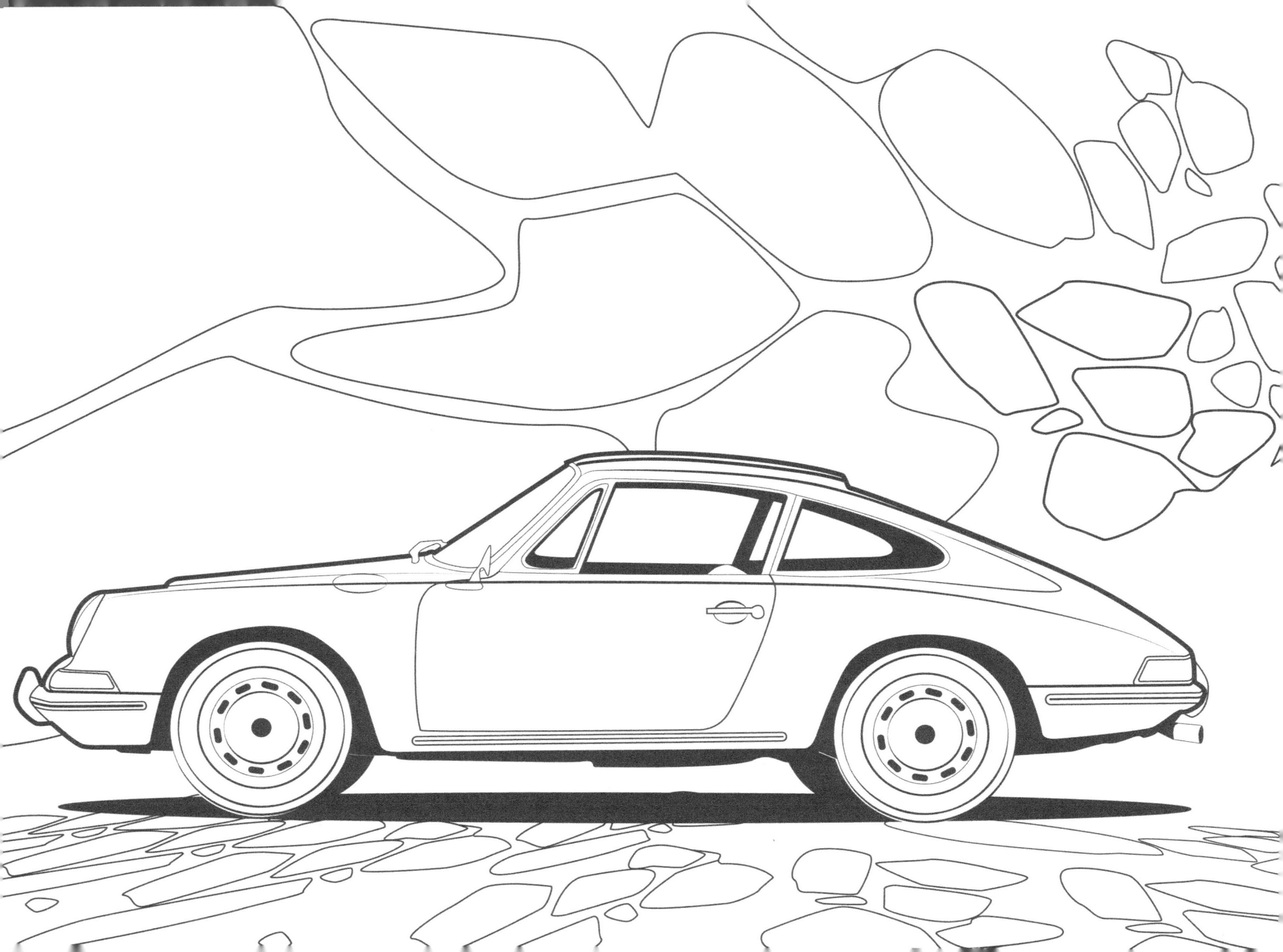

Can you name one of the most iconic sports cars ever produced? The 1st generation model had a distinctive eye catching design. This model has essentially standardized the companies overall look through models of today.

Top speed: 132 mph

0-60 time: 9 seconds

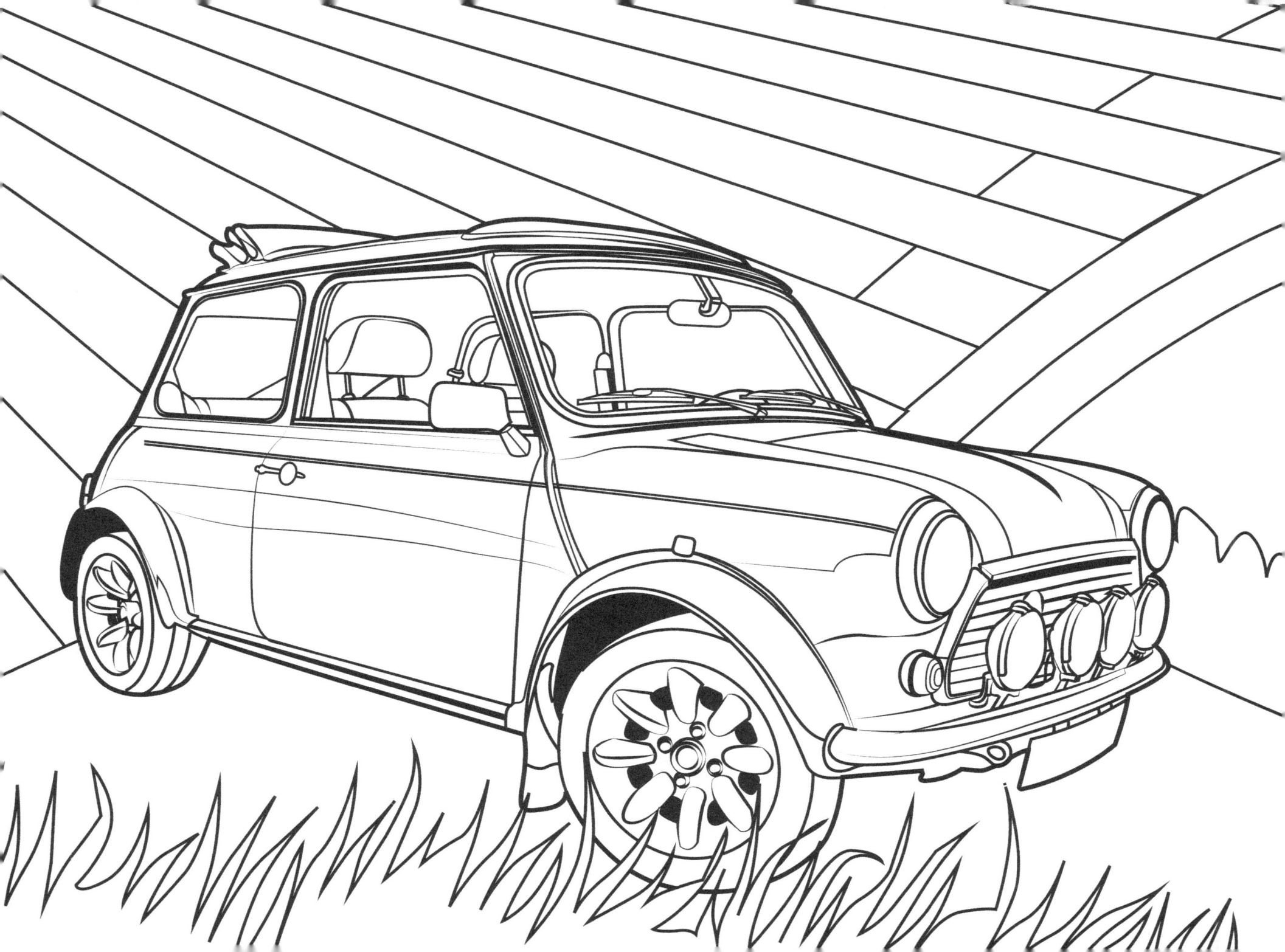

Can you name this highly recogonizable British icon? This performance car was unique in both its design and in its go-kart like handling abilities, which led to much success in rally races during the 1960s. It is also known for its distinctive front wheel drive layout allowing for 80% of the vehicle to be passenger room.

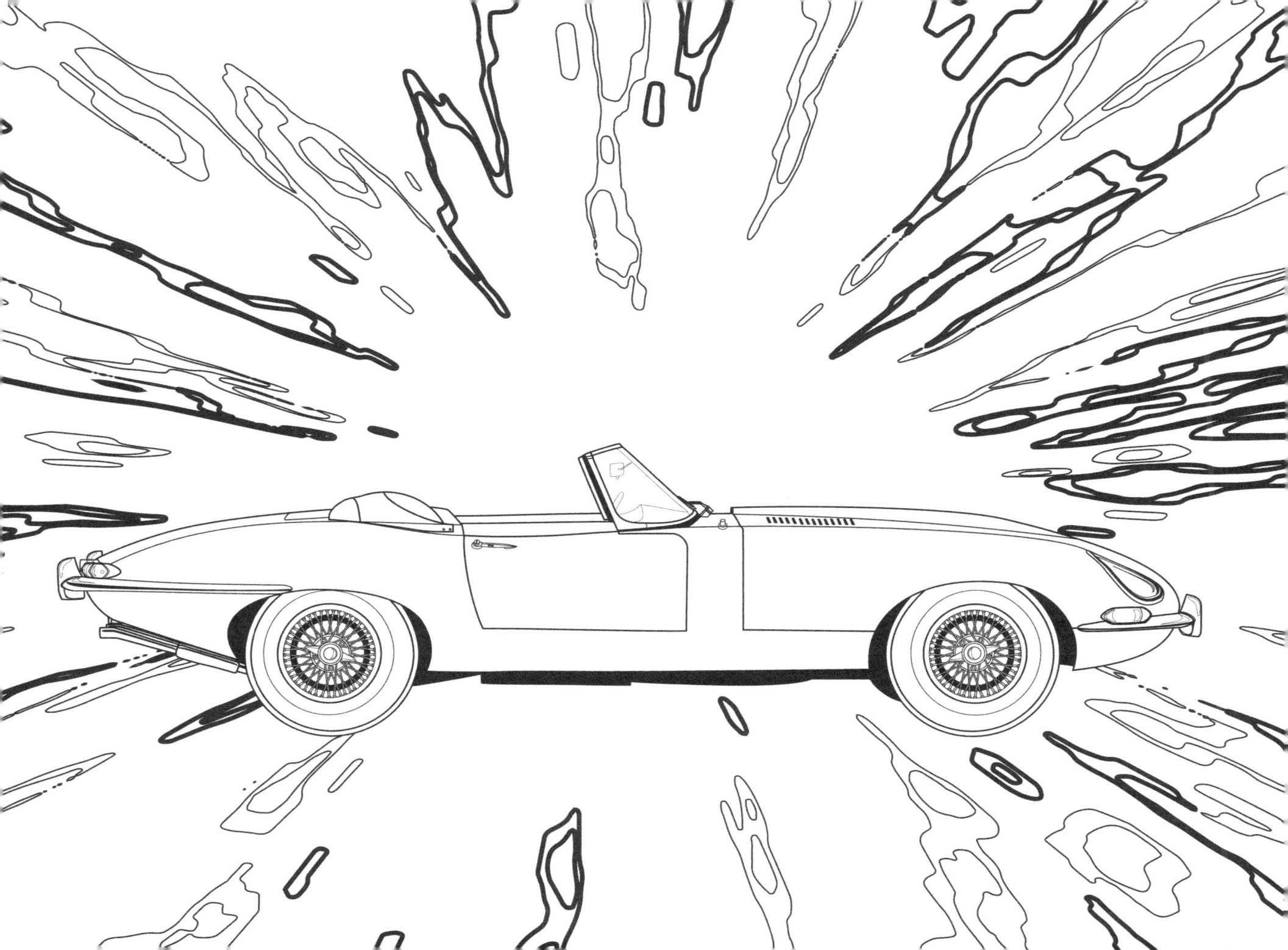

Can you name this British icon? Combining high performance, beautiful design and competitive pricing this vehicle went unrivaled in 1964. It was Capable of displaying an impressive 0-60mph acceleration time in just 7 seconds and a top speed of 150 mph.
Current value: $500,000- $5 million

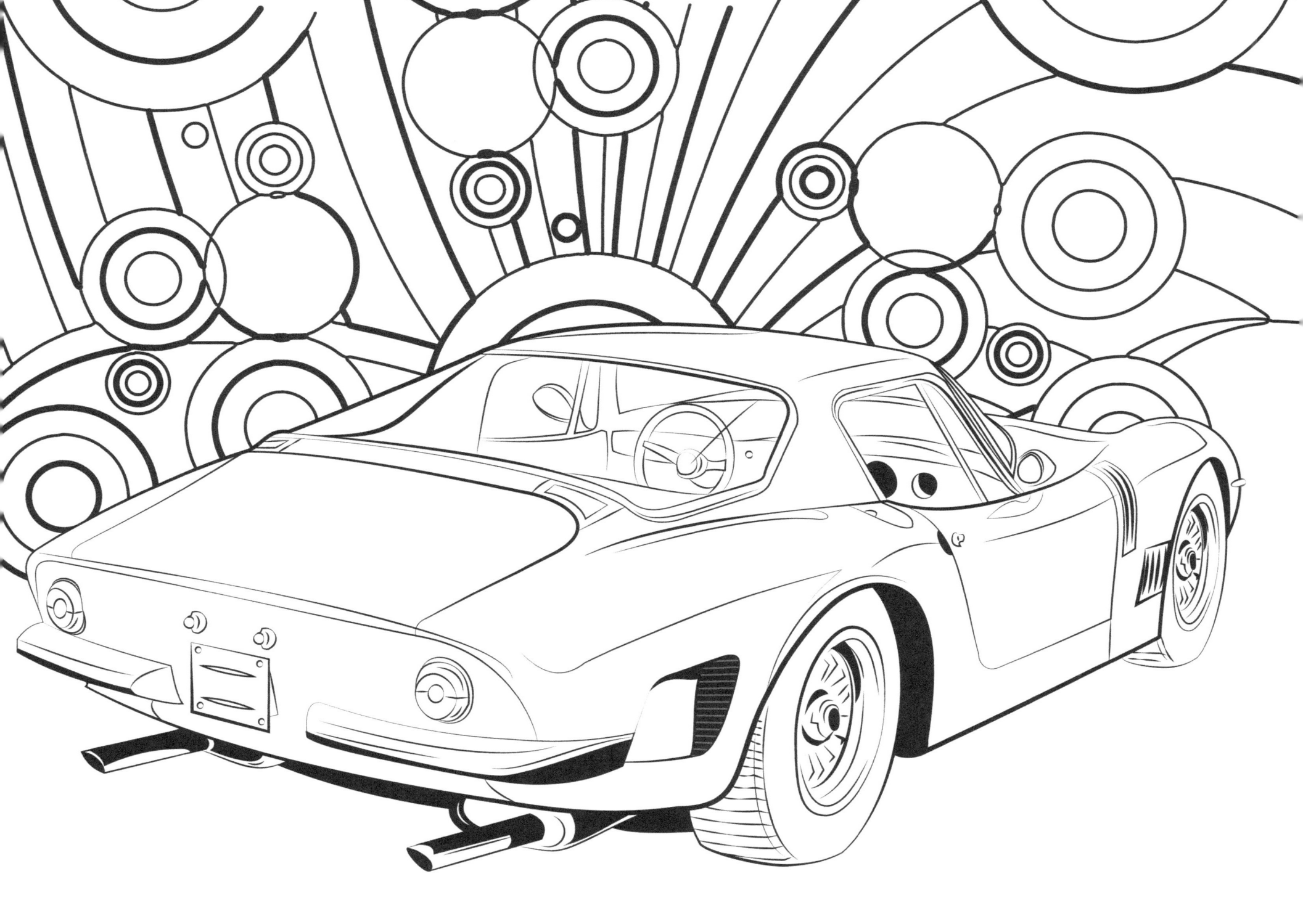

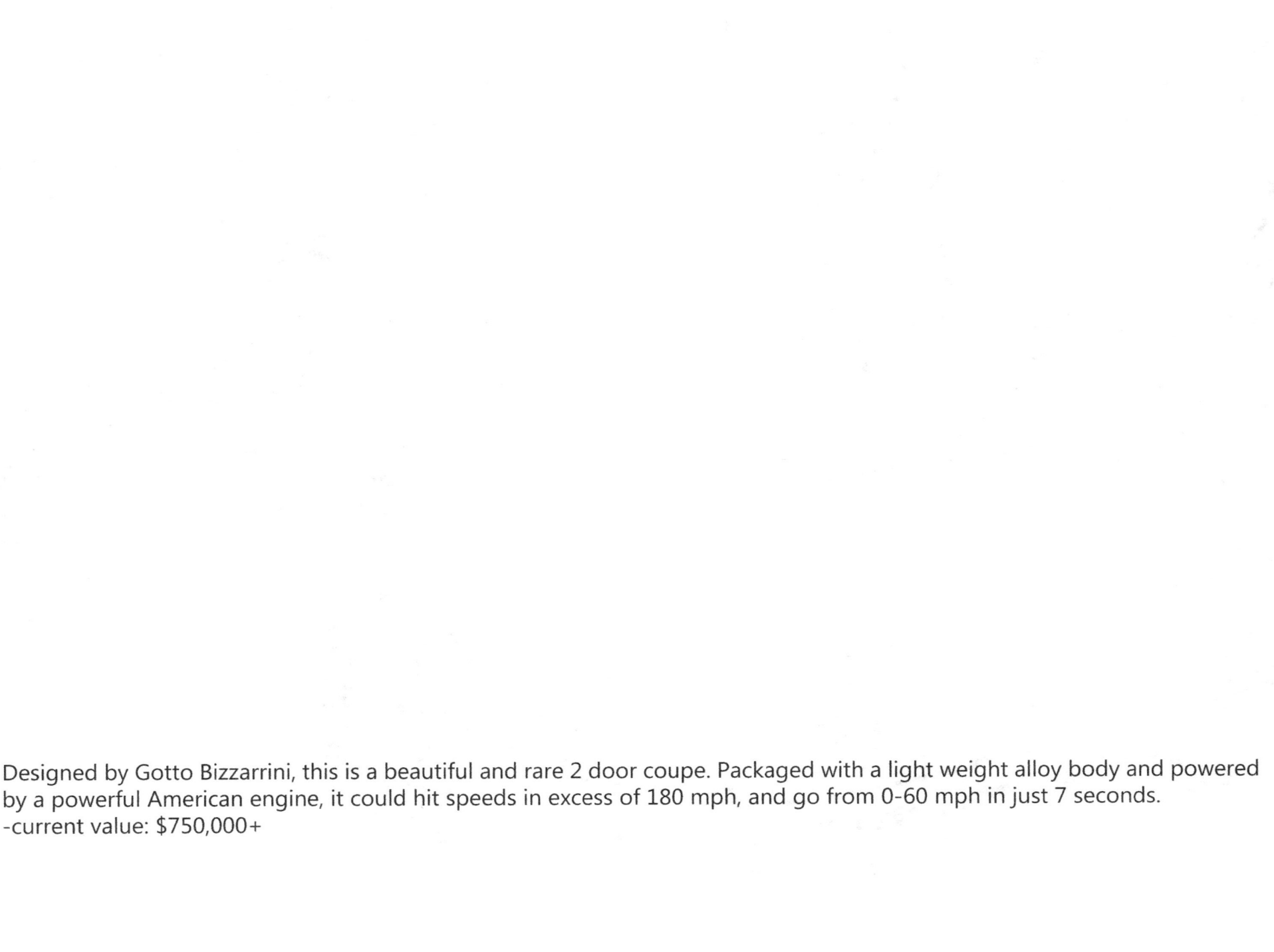

Designed by Gotto Bizzarrini, this is a beautiful and rare 2 door coupe. Packaged with a light weight alloy body and powered by a powerful American engine, it could hit speeds in excess of 180 mph, and go from 0-60 mph in just 7 seconds.
-current value: $750,000+

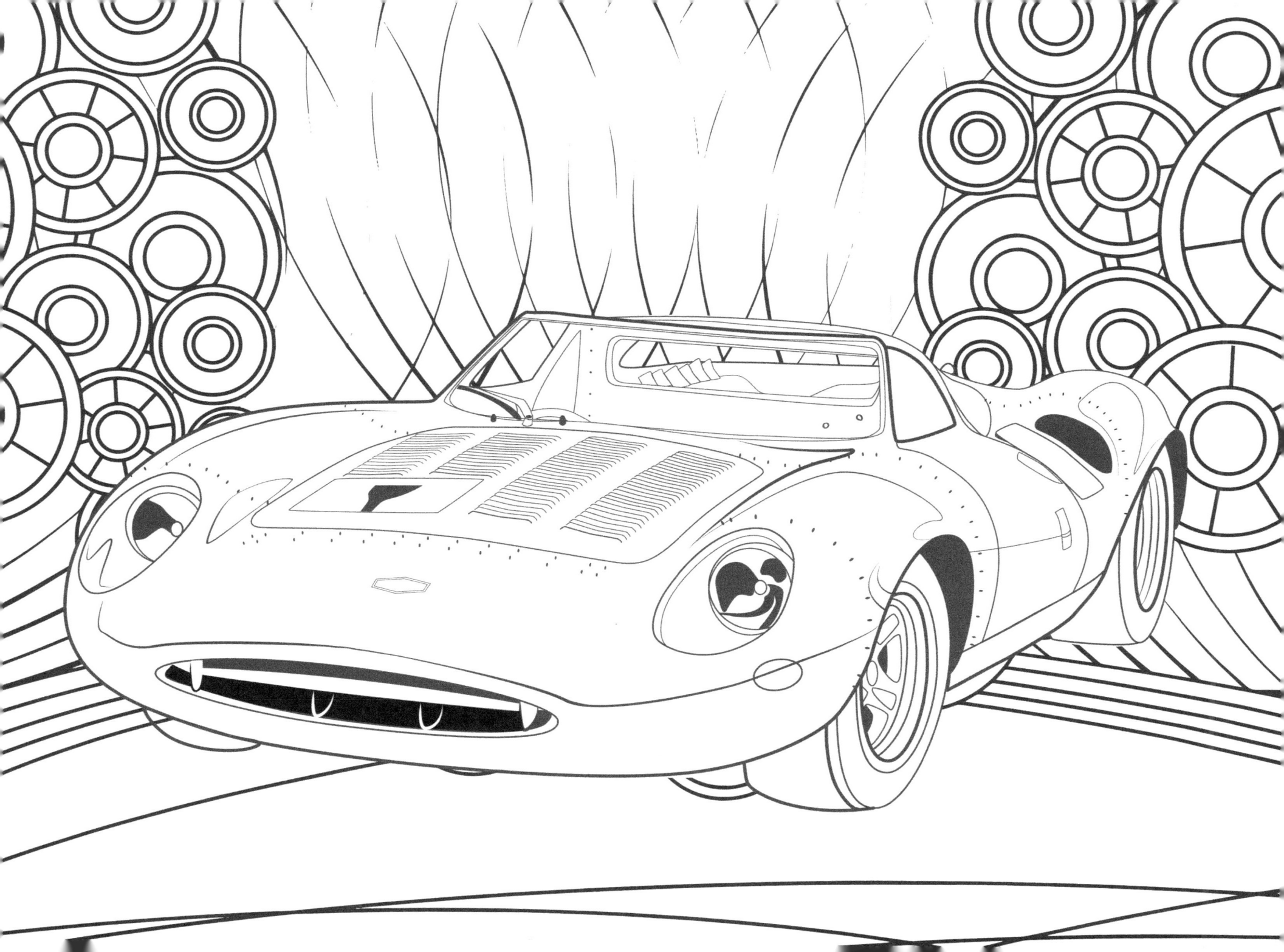

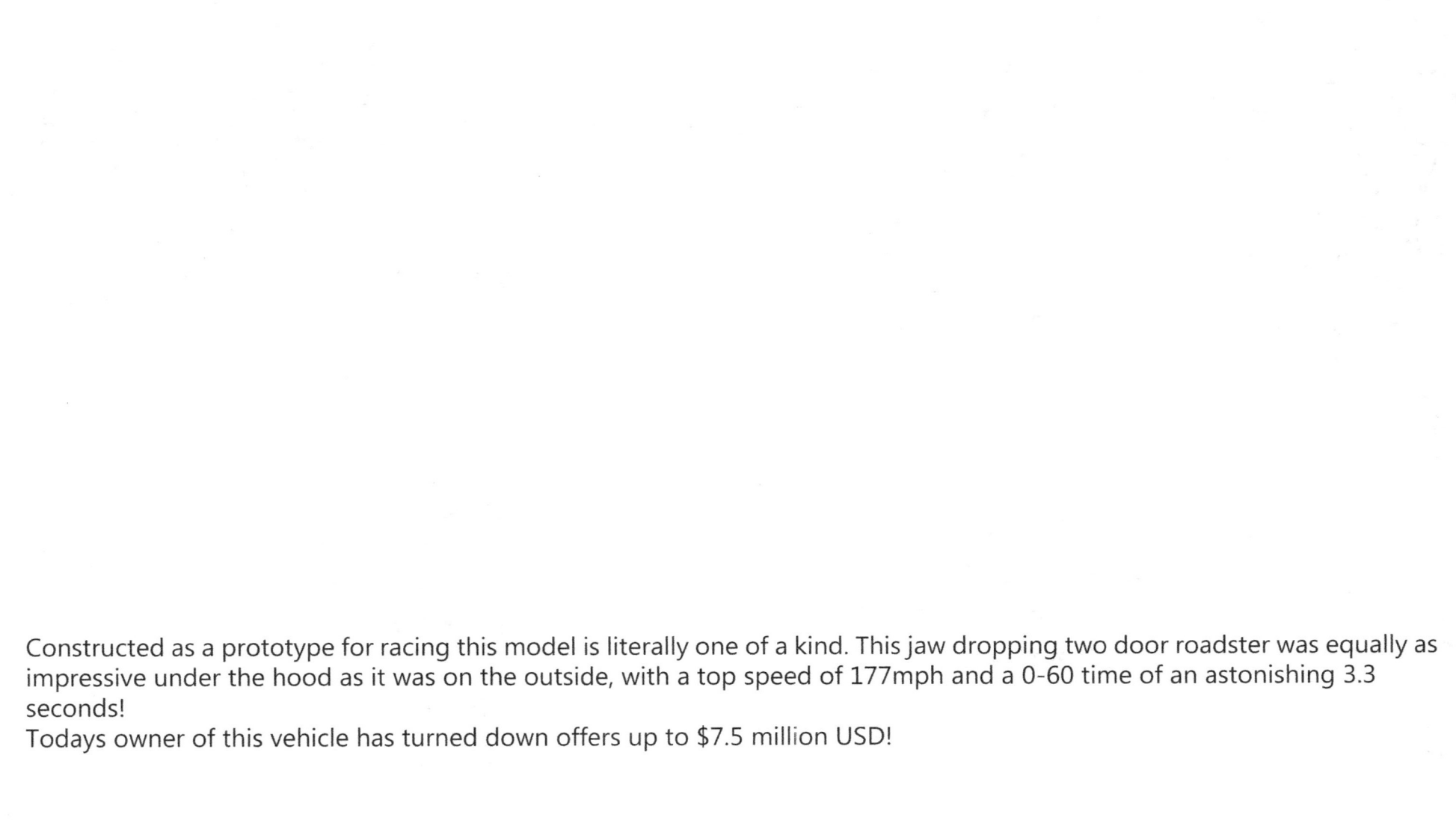

Constructed as a prototype for racing this model is literally one of a kind. This jaw dropping two door roadster was equally as impressive under the hood as it was on the outside, with a top speed of 177mph and a 0-60 time of an astonishing 3.3 seconds!

Todays owner of this vehicle has turned down offers up to $7.5 million USD!

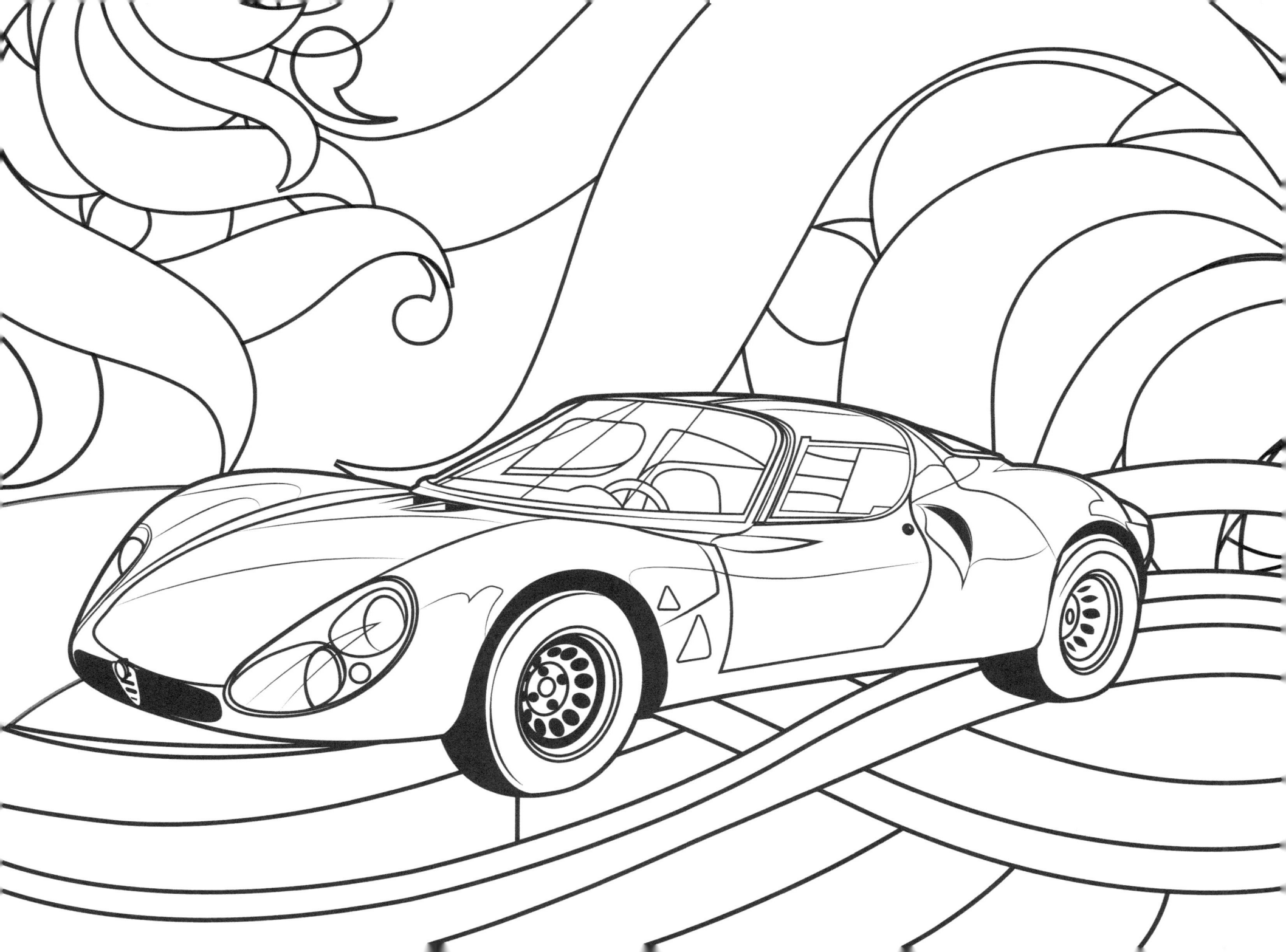

Can you name this Italian classic?

It was released in 1967 with a top speed of 160 mph as well as an off the line time of 5.5 seconds. Impressive in both design and performance it was also the most expensive car available to the public at $17,000 USD new. Today's worth over $10,000,000 USD

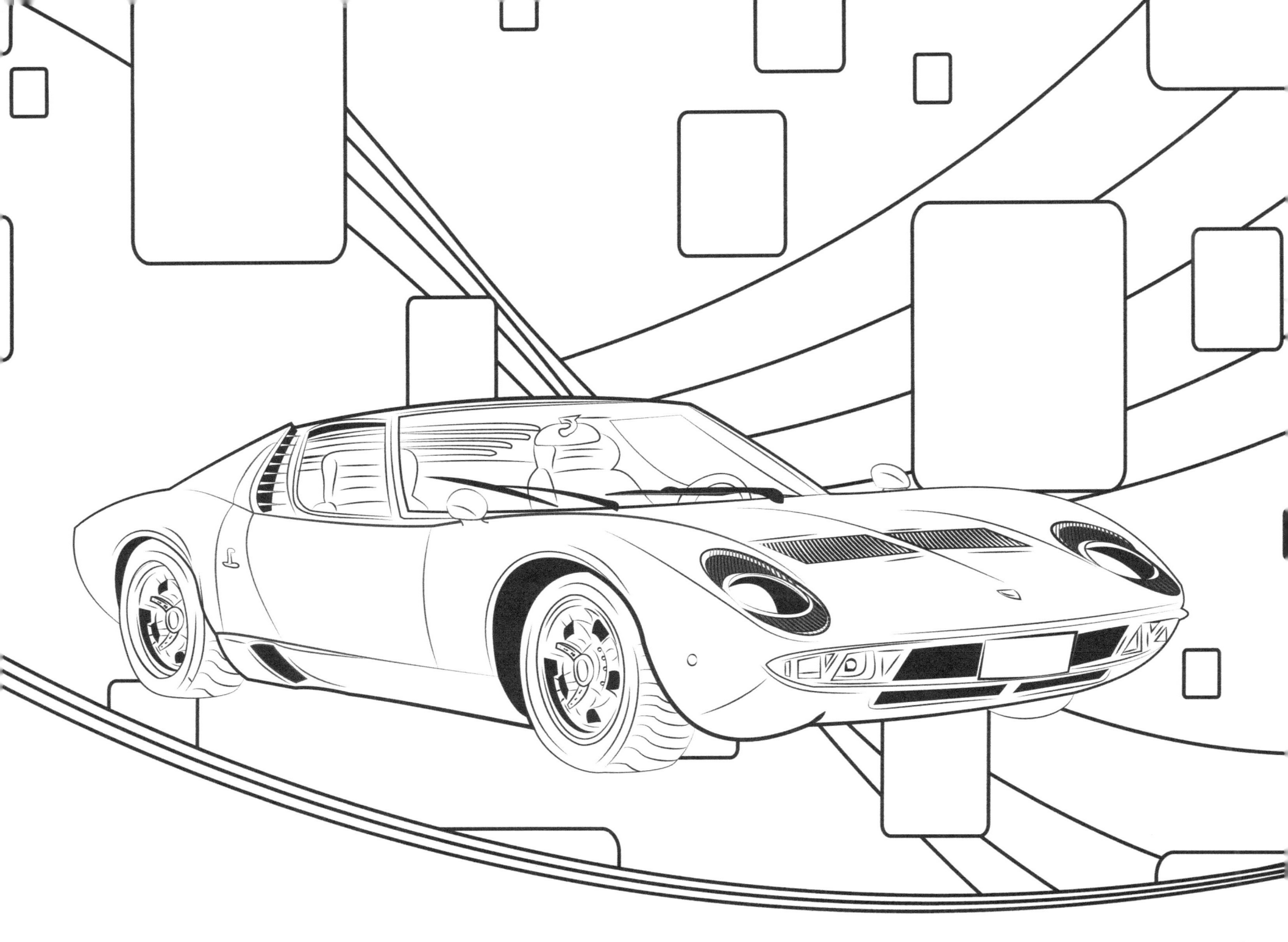

The 2nd generation of this model shared the same body design and V12 engine as its predecessor but included many upgrades. For the first time it included optional air conditioning as well as chrome trim around the windows, locking glove box as well as an engine overhaul to gain an additional 20 horsepower.
- top speed: 168 mph
- 0-60 in 5.5 seconds
- current value: approx $500,000 USD

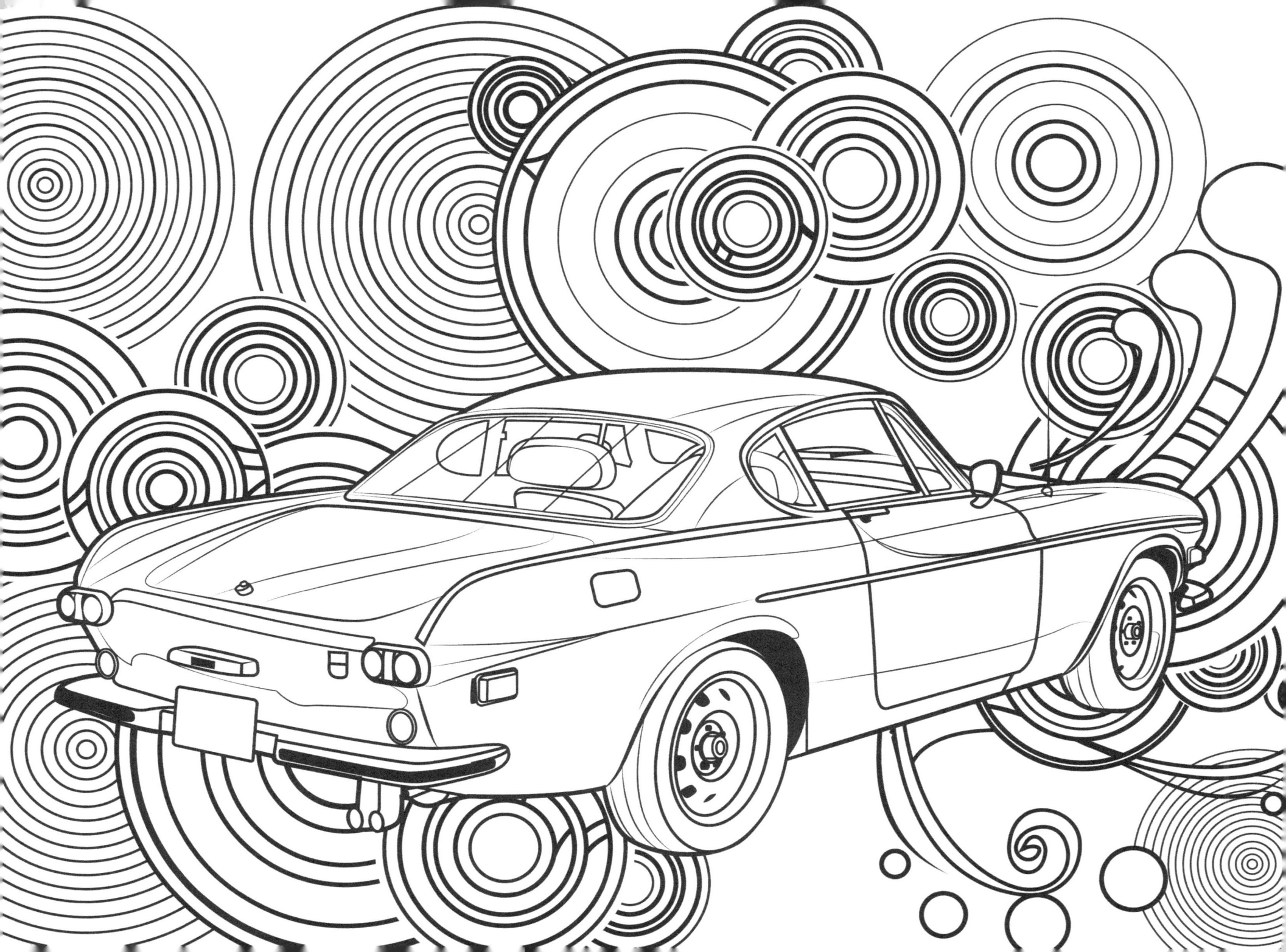

A stylish touring car designed as a sports car, this icon had the looks and durability.
It's the world record holder for highest mileage driven by a single vehicle with an astounding 3million+ miles. This model is
a company fan favorite to this day.

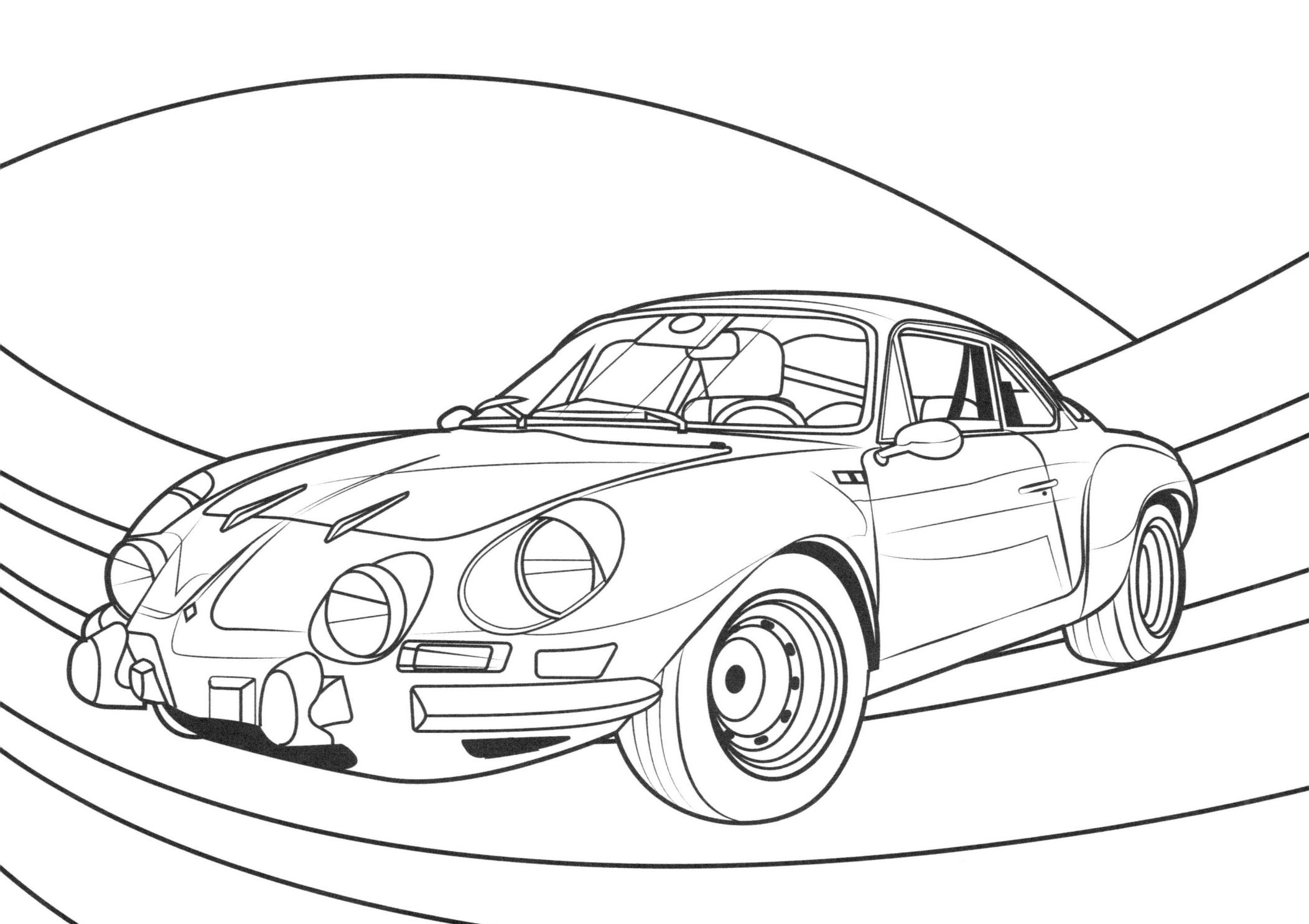

Can you name this car? One of the most successful rally cars of its time, this French icon captured numerous rally awards. With a design that really showed off the aggressive capabilities under the hood, this masterpiece introduced the world to the next level of rally cars.
- 0-60 acceleration time: 7.1 seconds
- top speed: 134 mph
- current price value: $110,000+

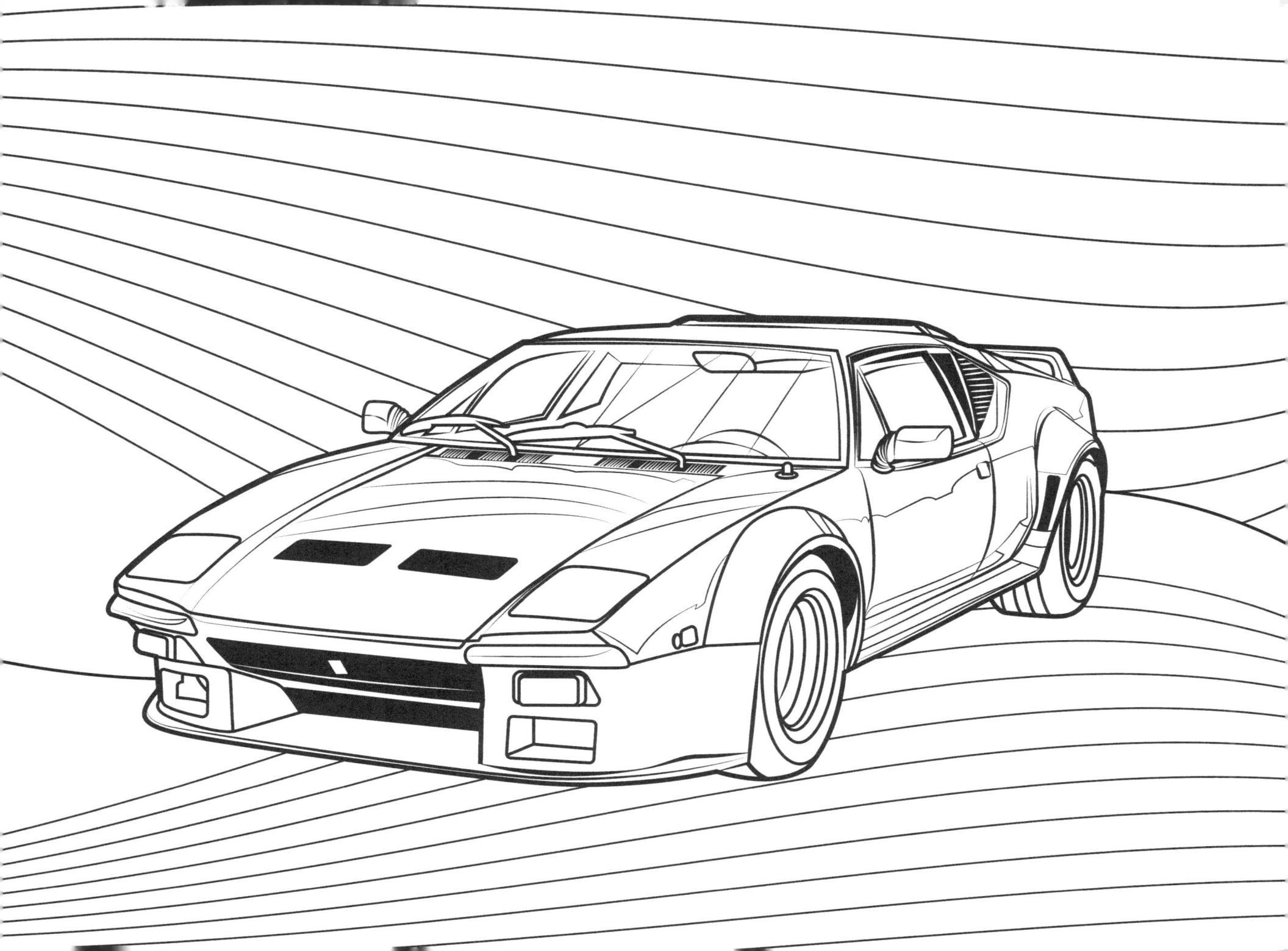

Can you name this italian beast? Hint: Its name is italian for Panther, and it is a rare rally car with capabilities off the line of reaching 60 mph in just 5.5 seconds. Italian design meets American muscle here with its V8 powered American made engine.
-price: $330,000+

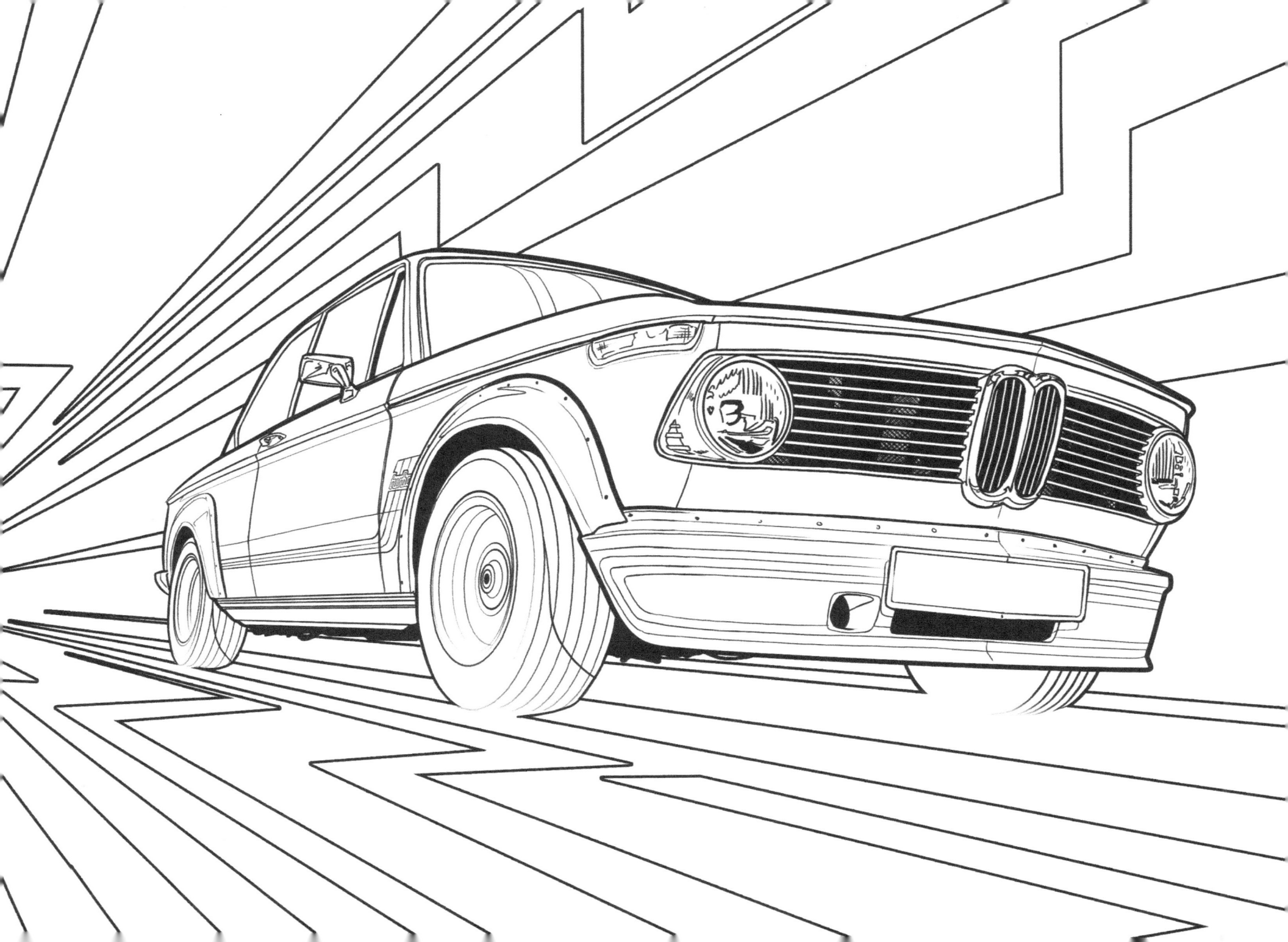

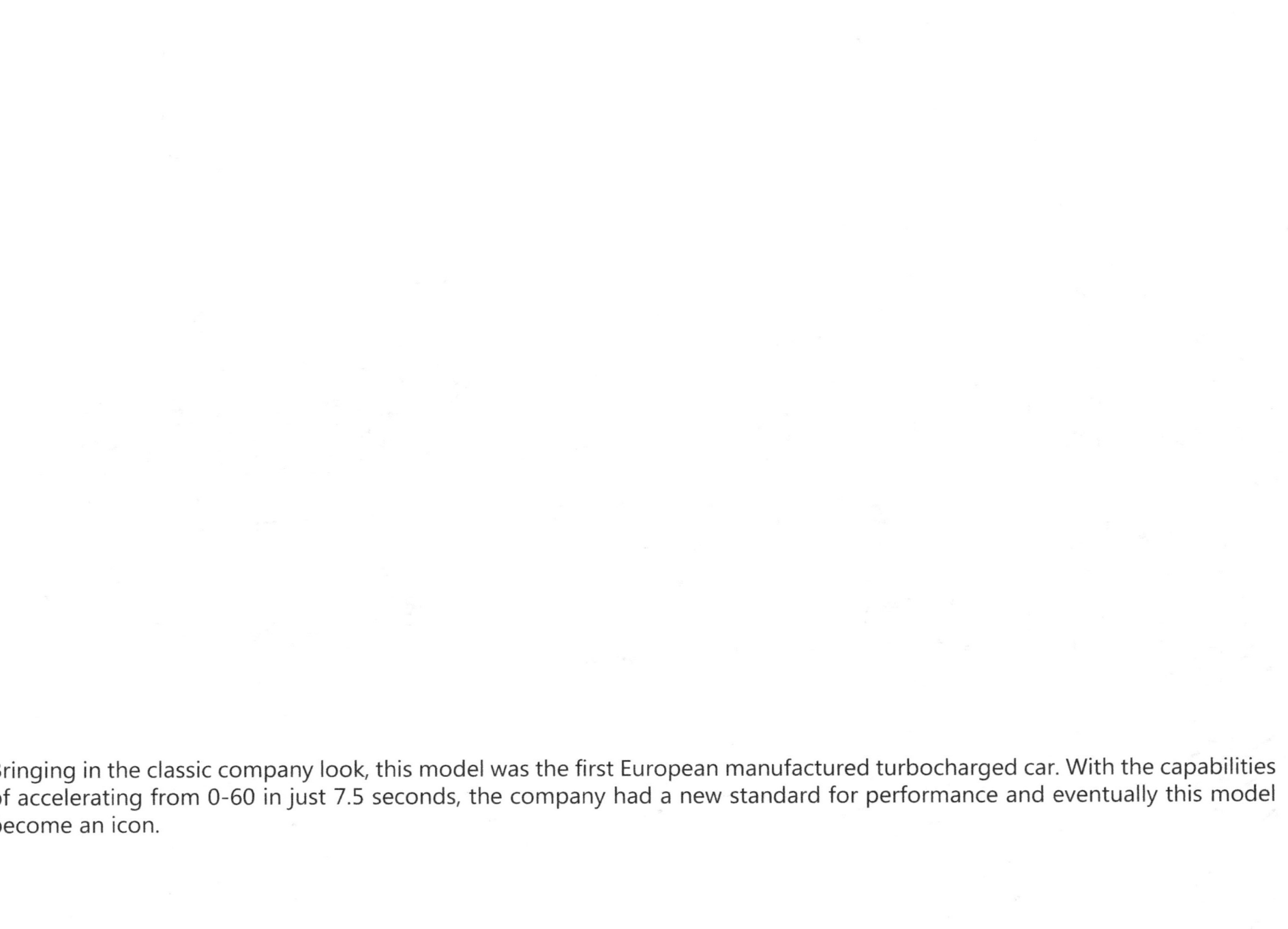

Bringing in the classic company look, this model was the first European manufactured turbocharged car. With the capabilities of accelerating from 0-60 in just 7.5 seconds, the company had a new standard for performance and eventually this model become an icon.

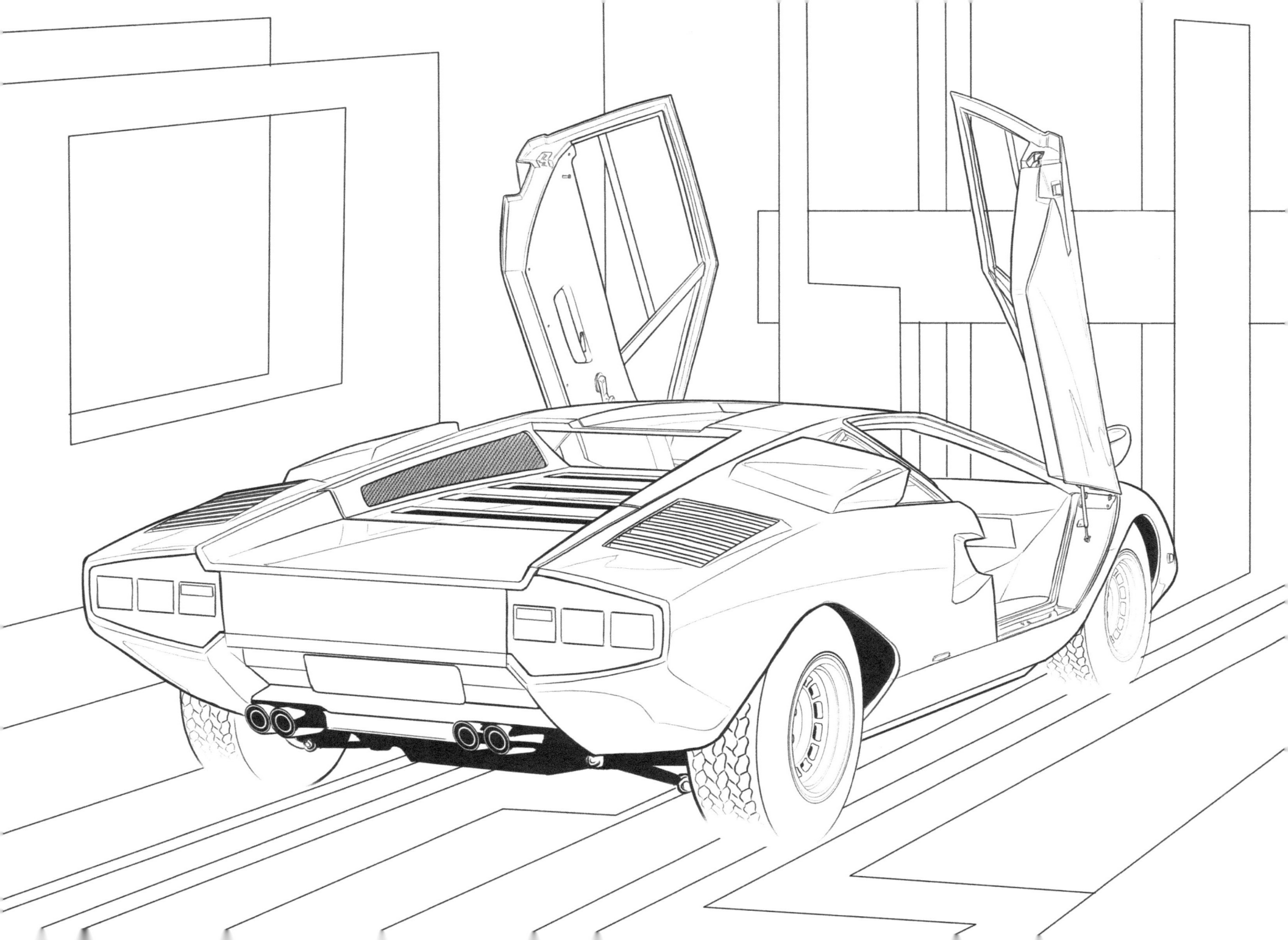

A narrow bodied bullet pushing the needle on the speedometer to 196 mph and an off the line time from 0-60 in 5.6 seconds, this highly sought after Italian icon not only performed like a monster but looked the part while doing it. Can you name this model?
- Current value ranges from $450,000-1.5 million

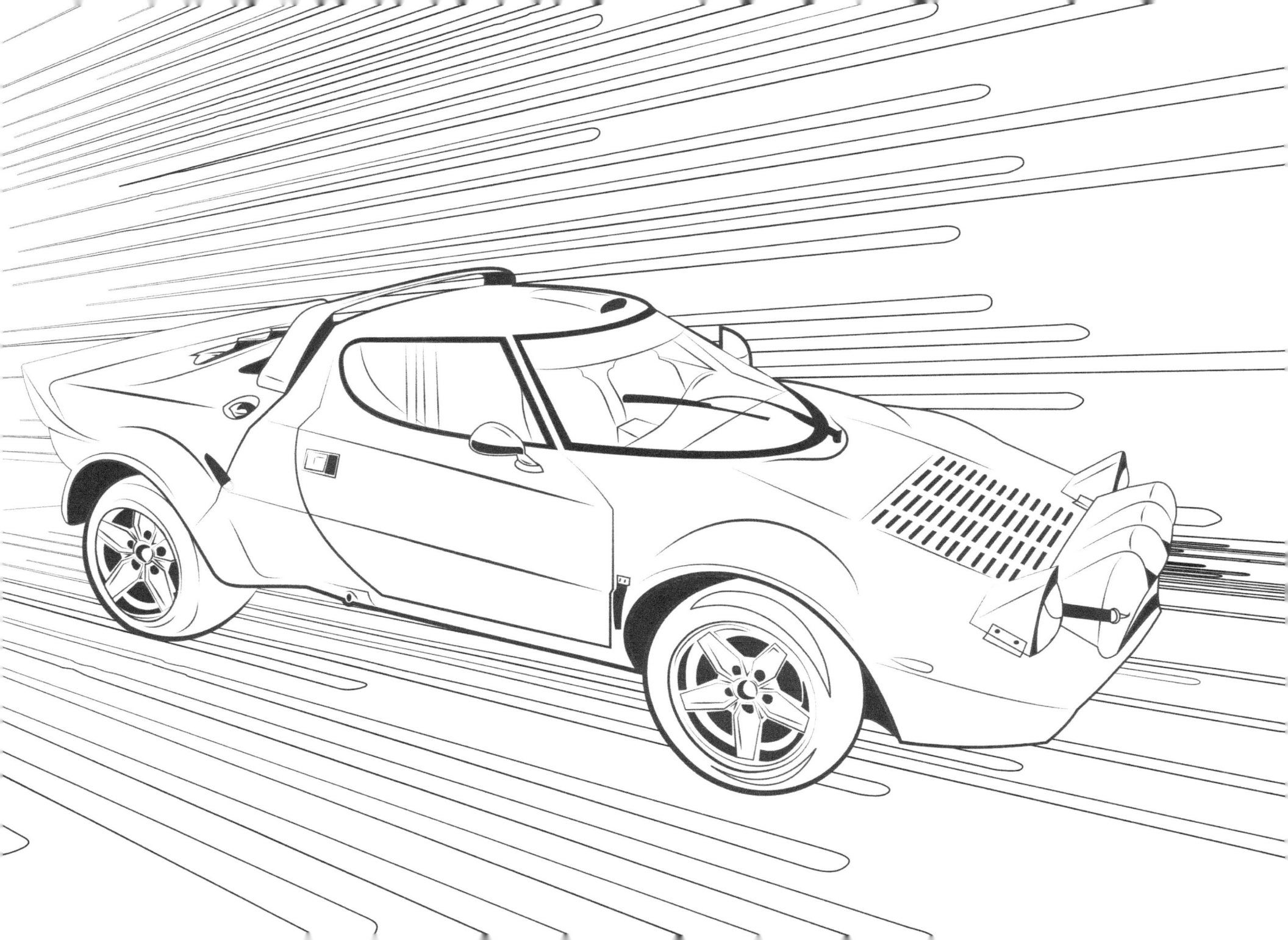

Arguably the most legendary rally car in history, this model was an eye catcher and a performer. It's featured wedge shape design, wrap around windshield and short wheelbase it easily stood out from the crowd but in a good way. Under the hood was a fitted V6 engine.
- award winning rally racer
- 0-60 in 7 seconds
-top speed: 143+
- currently valued at $250,000-500,000

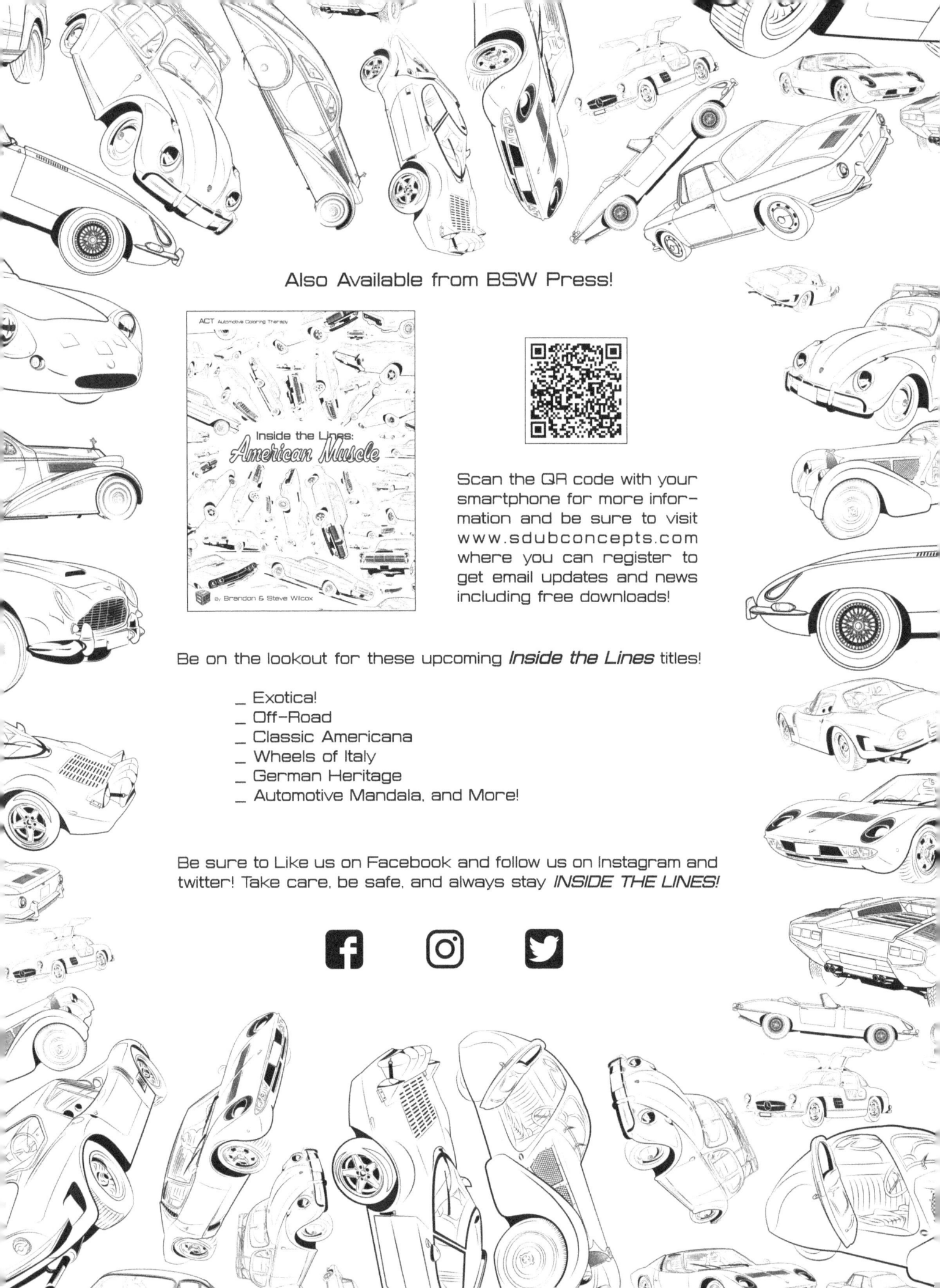

Also Available from BSW Press!

ACT Automotive Coloring Therapy

Inside the Lines:
American Muscle

by Brandon & Steve Wilcox

Scan the QR code with your smartphone for more information and be sure to visit www.sdubconcepts.com where you can register to get email updates and news including free downloads!

Be on the lookout for these upcoming *Inside the Lines* titles!

_ Exotica!
_ Off-Road
_ Classic Americana
_ Wheels of Italy
_ German Heritage
_ Automotive Mandala, and More!

Be sure to Like us on Facebook and follow us on Instagram and twitter! Take care, be safe, and always stay *INSIDE THE LINES!*

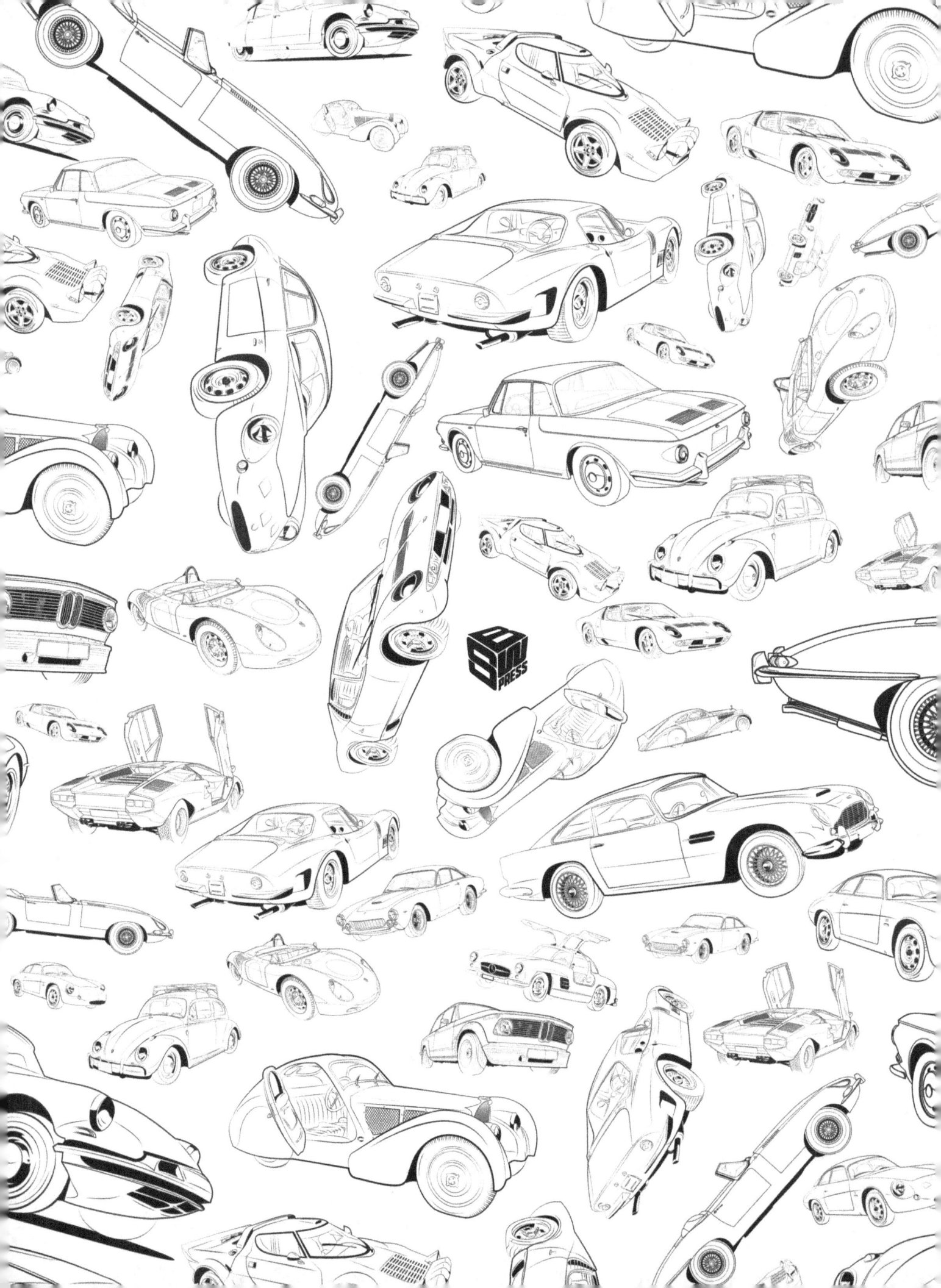